3 9082 12914 7610

DATE DUE

BRODART, CO.   Cat. No. 23-221-003

DISCIPLINE EQUALS FREEDOM

DISCIPLINE EQUALS FREEDOM: FIELD MANUAL

JOCKO WILLINK

ST. MARTIN'S PRESS
NEW YORK

DISCIPLINE EQUALS FREEDOM: FIELD MANUAL. Copyright © 2017
by Jocko Willink. All rights reserved. Printed in the
United States of America. For information, address St.
Martin's Press, 175 Fifth Avenue, New York, N.Y. 10010.

www.stmartins.com

Produced by the Stonesong Press, LLC
Interior design by Peter Romeo, Wooly Head Design
Photos by Jocko Willink
Grappling photos by Courtney Henderson: pp 30—31, 40—41,
54—55, 118—19, 124—25, 128—29.

The Library of Congress Cataloging-in-Publication Data is
available upon request.

ISBN 978-1-250-15694-5 (hardcover)
ISBN 978-1-250-18471-9 (signed edition)
ISBN 978-1-250-15695-2 (ebook)

Our books may be purchased in bulk for promotional,
educational, or business use. Please contact your local
bookseller or the Macmillan Corporate and Premium Sales
Department at 1-800-221-7945, extension 5442, or by email
at MacmillanSpecialMarkets@macmillan.com.

First Edition: October 2017

10 9 8 7 6 5 4 3 2 1

CONTENTS

This book is dedicated to

Marc Lee,
Mike Monsoor,
and
Ryan Job,

from SEAL Team Three, Task Unit Bruiser,
who lived, and fought, and died
as warriors.

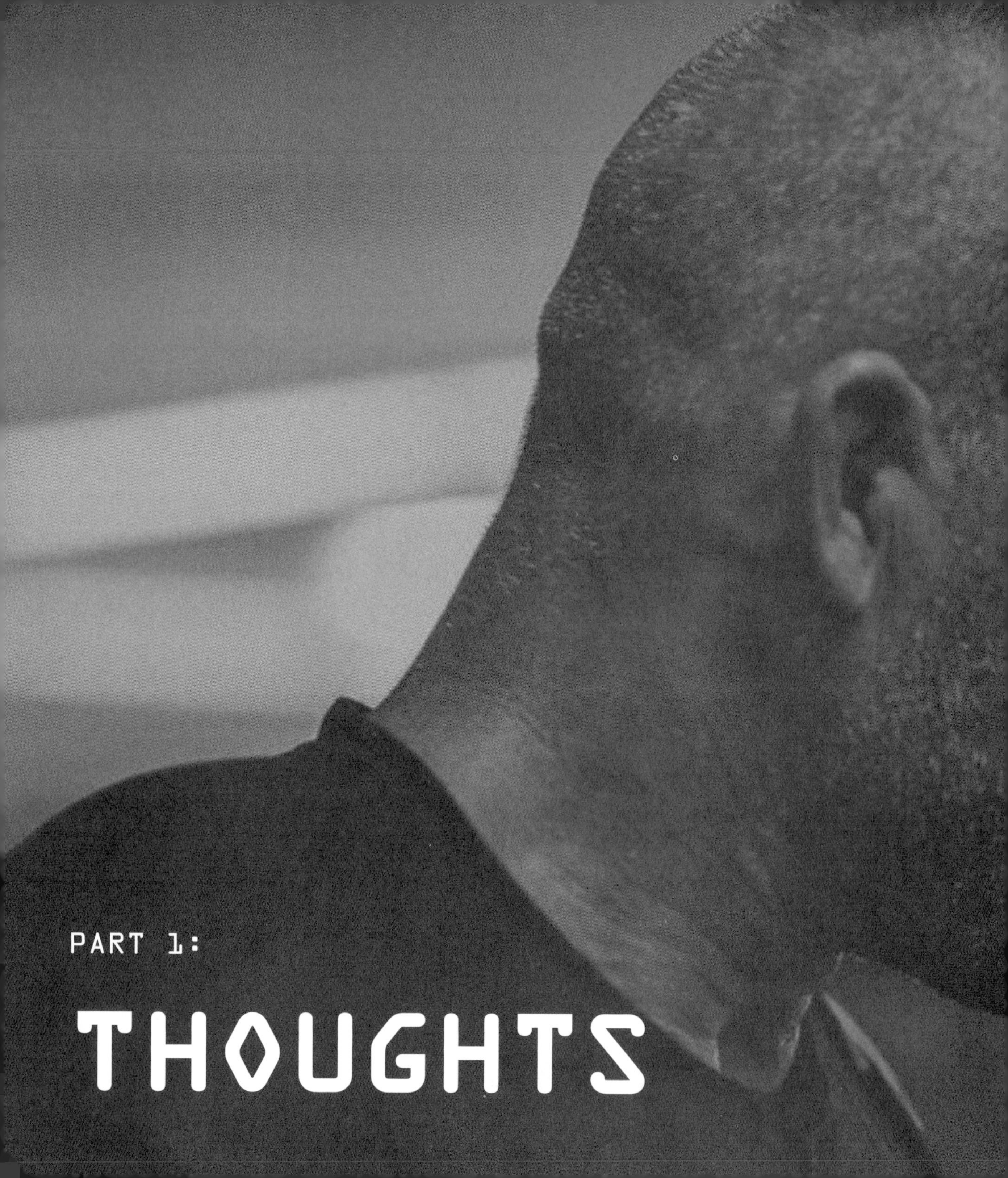

PART 1:

THOUGHTS

THE WAY

People look for the shortcut. The hack.

And if you came here looking for that:
You won't find it.

The shortcut is a lie.
The hack doesn't get you there.

And if you want to take the easy road, it won't
take you to where you want to be:
Stronger. Smarter. Faster. Healthier. Better.

FREE.

To reach goals and overcome obstacles
and become the best version of you possible
will not happen by itself. It will not
happen cutting corners, taking shortcuts,
or looking for the easy way.

THERE IS NO EASY WAY.

OF DISCIPLINE

There is only hard work, late nights, early mornings, practice, rehearsal, repetition, study, sweat, blood, toil, frustration, and discipline. DISCIPLINE.

THERE MUST BE DISCIPLINE.

Discipline: The root of all good qualities. The driver of daily execution. The core principle that overcomes laziness and lethargy and excuses. Discipline defeats the infinite excuses that say: Not today, not now, I need a rest, I will do it tomorrow.

What's the hack? How do you become stronger, smarter, faster, healthier? How do you become better? How do you achieve true freedom?

There is only one way.

THE WAY OF DISCIPLINE.

WHY

Why?
Over and over and over again, I am asked: Why?
What drives me.
When I was younger, I was preparing for war.
I knew that somewhere out there,
another man was also preparing.
That man was my enemy.
He was working, training, planning, and preparing
to meet me on the battlefield.
I didn't know when.
I didn't know where.
But I knew that at some point: We would meet.
And I wanted to be ready.
Ready mentally.
Ready physically.
Ready emotionally.
So I trained. And I prepared. And I did
everything I could to be ready for that day.
When I became a leader, I took the same approach.
To prepare my men in the same way:
To train brutally and without mercy
so we could fight brutally and without mercy.
And the day came.
We met the enemy on the battlefield.

We were ready and we fought
    and we won.
Then one day, it was over.
I was no longer a soldier; no longer a leader of men.
    I was no longer preparing myself or my men
    for war.
So. What drives me now?
The answer is simple:
    The men that did not come home.

Marc and Mikey and Ryan.

But it is not only them.
There are others.
Hundreds more.
    Thousands more.
        Countless more.
Who fought and died to give me the gift of freedom.
    And for them,
        I will make every day—every minute—every
        second—I will make it all count.
I will live to honor their sacrifice—
        A life worthy of the price they paid,
                                for me,
                                for us.

I will not let them down.

WHERE DOES

Where does discipline come from?
This is a simple answer.
Discipline comes from within.
Discipline is an internal force.

Sure, you can have discipline imposed on
you by a person, like a drill instructor,
or that self-help guru on TV, but the
reality is: He won't give you real discipline.

Because that external discipline is
not strong. It will not survive.
It cannot stand on its own.
What you are looking for,

what you need, is **SELF-DISCIPLINE**.

Self-discipline, as the very term implies,
comes from the SELF. YOU.
It comes when you make a decision
to be disciplined.
When you make a decision to be better.

DISCIPLINE COME FROM?

When you make a decision to do more, to BE more.
Self-discipline comes when you decide to make
a mark on the world.
If you don't think you are disciplined:

It is because you haven't decided to be
disciplined. **YET**.
It is because you haven't created it. **YET**.
You haven't become it. **YET**.
So where does it come from?
It comes from *you*.
So make the decision.
Make the commitment.
Become the discipline—embrace its cold and
relentless power.
And it will make you better and stronger and
smarter and faster and healthier than anything
else. And most important:
It will make you free.

OVERCOMING PROCRASTINATION:

People want to know how to stop laziness.
They want to know how to stop
procrastination.

They have an idea in their head...
Maybe even a *vision*.

But they don't know where to start—so they ask.
And they say: "Where do I start?"
"When is the best time to start?"
And I have a simple answer:

HERE and **NOW**.

That's it.
You want to improve?
You want to get better?
You want to get on a workout program or a clean
diet or start a new business?
You want to write a book or make a movie or build
a house or a computer or an app?

WHEN AND WHERE TO START

Where do you start? You start right **HERE**.
When do you start? You start right **NOW**.
You initiate action.

You **GO**.

Here is the reality:
That idea isn't going to execute itself.
That book isn't going to write itself.
Those weights out in the gym—they aren't going to move themselves.

YOU HAVE TO DO IT.

And you have to do it now. So stop thinking about it. Stop dreaming about it.
Stop researching every aspect of it and reading all about it and debating the pros and cons of it...
Start doing it.
Take that first step and Make It Happen.
GET AFTER IT.

HERE and **NOW**.

THE PERSON

People are not who you want them to be. Kill your idols. Sure there are things we can learn from people—but people aren't going to be what you think they are—what they should be.

People, even those people you have put up on a pedestal, are going to be faulted, weak, egomaniacal, condescending. They are going to be lazy, entitled, shortsighted. They will not be perfect. Far from it.

That's fine. Learn from their weaknesses. Of course: Learn from their strengths and mimic and copy them in what they do well. But equally as important: Learn from their faults.

See what not to do.

YOU CAN CONTROL

Because you can't control other people. You can't make them what you want them to be. You can't make them who you want them to be.

The only person you can control is you. So focus on making yourself who you want you to be:

Faster. Stronger. Smarter. More humble. **Less ego.**

Discipline your body. Free your mind.
Get up early, and go.
Get after it and you will become the person you want to be.
And you become that person through:

One. Small. Decision. At. A. Time.

MIND

When people think of the words "mind control,"
they think of people controlling the minds of
other people. Not me.
I think about controlling my own mind.
Sure, we are physical beings, and we must
obviously embrace our physicality.
But we *are* our minds.
And I'm not going to go philosophical on what
that means and where the "YOU" actually is —
whether it is a soul or your brain or your heart
or some other conjured-up place.
What I do know is this: You, your mind, the thing
that is reading and comprehending these words
right now, that IS YOU.
And you can control it. You are the machine, and
you can control it.
People ask me, "How do I get tougher?"
BE TOUGHER.
"How can I wake up early in the morning?"
WAKE UP EARLY.
"How can I work out consistently every day?"
WORK OUT CONSISTENTLY EVERY DAY.

CONTROL

"How can I stop eating sugar?"
     STOP EATING SUGAR.
You can even control your emotions:
"How can I stop missing that girl or guy or whoever broke up with me?"
     STOP MISSING THEM.
You have control over your mind. You just have to assert it.
You have to decide that you are going to be in control, that you are going to do what YOU want to do.
Weakness doesn't get a vote.
          Laziness doesn't get a vote.
               Sadness doesn't get a vote.
                    Frustration doesn't get a vote.
                              Negativity

          DOESN'T GET A VOTE!
Your temper doesn't get a vote.

So next time you are feeling weak or lazy or soft or emotional, tell those feelings they don't get a vote.

You are declaring martial law on your mind:

MIND CONTROL.

Impose what you want on your brain:

DISCIPLINE.
POWER.
POSITIVITY.
WILL.

And use that Mind Control to move
your life where you want it to be:
stronger, faster, smarter, quicker, friendlier,
more helpful, more driven.
Don't let your mind control you.
Control your mind. And then you can:

SET IT FREE.

WEAKNESS

Do I have weakness?
I am nothing but weakness.
I am not naturally strong, or fast, or flexible.
I am certainly not the smartest person
in the world.

I get emotional over stupid things.
I eat the wrong foods.
I don't sleep enough.
I procrastinate and I waste time.
I care too much about meaningless things and not
enough about important things.
My ego is too big.
My mind is too small,
often trapped inside itself.

Now all that being said, I have a saying: A
person's strength is often their
biggest weakness.
But, their weaknesses can become strengths.
Me? I am weak, in all those ways, I am weak.

BUT
           I don't accept that.

I don't accept that I am what I am and that
"that" is what I am doomed to be.
NO. I do not accept that.
I'm fighting.
I'm always fighting. I'm struggling and I'm
scraping and kicking and clawing at those
weaknesses—to change them. To stop them.
Some days I win. But some days I don't.
But each and every day: I get back up
           and I move forward.
               With my fists clenched.
Toward the battle. Toward the struggle.
And I fight with everything I've got:
To overcome those weaknesses and those shortfalls
and those flaws as I strive to be just a
               little bit better today
               than I was yesterday...

STRESS

First of all, and I don't mean to minimize the
stress people face, but:
Imagine what Eugene Sledge went through on
Peleliu and the tens of thousands of Marines
there who suffered unimaginable horror.
Imagine David Hackworth assaulting enemy
positions in Korea, wounded over and over again on
the line, still going back for more.
Imagine the poet warrior Alan Seeger in
World War One getting ready to go over the top
and make his rendezvous with death..
Imagine the thousands of warriors who
have gone before you, who have stood and faced
evil and death.

And now imagine you. I used to do this myself
while in Iraq facing stress.
Yes, we took casualties, and yes
it was awful and heartbreaking and
every bit as wretched as I could imagine.

But warriors have faced much much worse:
The Battle of the Somme, or Gettysburg, or the
Battle of the Bulge, or the Chosin Reservoir.
Humans can withstand almost inconceivable
stress—and you can too.
So that is your first step: Gain perspective.
And to do that you must do something critical in
many situations: Detach.
Whatever problems or stress you are experiencing,
detach from them.
Stress is generally caused by what you
can't control.

> The worst thing about incoming artillery fire
> is you can't control it. It is happening and
> you just have to accept it. Don't stress
> about things you can't control.

If the stress is something that you can control
and you are not, that is a lack of discipline and
a lack of ownership.
Get control of it. Impose your will to make it
happen. Solve the problem. Relieve the stress.

If the stress is something you can't control
                                    Embrace it
                    You can't control it, but—
How can you look at it from a different angle
        How can you use it to your advantage

        I couldn't control the chaos of combat

                            I had to embrace it

                        I had to figure out a way
                        to take advantage of it

                        Make it into your ally

        So. Don't fight stress. Embrace it. Turn it on
itself. Use it to make yourself sharper and more
alert. Use it to make you think and learn and get
        better and smarter and more effective

            Use the stress to make you a better you

DESTROYER

Where does the switch come from? The overdrive.
The berserker mode. The full-on destroyer that
will not stop?
I think this is something that is learned.
And it is a hard lesson and not everyone gets it.
And it is an important lesson.
A critical one.
It is the thing that allows you to go the extra
distance.

To dig a little deeper.
To push a little harder.
To get after it.

And it actually takes two opposing forces to
bring it to life.
It takes both *emotion* and *logic* to reach your
maximum potential, to really give everything you
have, to go beyond your limits.

Because emotion and logic will
both reach their limitations.

MODE

And when one fails, you need to rely on the other.

When it just doesn't make any logical sense to go on, that's when you use your emotion, your anger, your frustration, your fear, to push further, to push you to say one thing: I don't stop.

When your feelings are screaming that you have had enough, when you think you are going to break emotionally, override that emotion with concrete logic and willpower that says one thing: I don't stop.

Fight weak emotions with the power of logic; fight the weakness of logic with the power of emotion.

And in the balance of those two, you will find the strength and the tenacity and the guts to say to yourself:

I. DON'T. STOP.

UNTIL

Something I saw in combat that I later tried to train out of people was the tendency to relax once the primary objective of a mission was complete. I tried to train that out of them because you can't relax until the entire mission is complete.

In training, we always attacked the platoons hard on their primary objective, but we always attacked them even harder after they left the main target, once the platoons were patrolling back to base, when their minds had already gone home and "turned off."

That's when we would bring it to them. Hit them from multiple angles with all kinds of mayhem. So they would develop the attitude and the muscle memory to keep going until the end.

And even when they got back to base, we would re-task them so they had to begin planning again. It wouldn't stop.

That's the mentality I wanted to instill in them:

It is never finished.

THE END

You always have more to do.
Another mission. Another task. Another goal.
And the enemy is always watching. Waiting.
Looking for that moment of weakness.
Looking for you to exhale, set your weapon down, and
close your eyes, even just for a moment.
And that's when they attack.
So don't be finished.

Be starting. Be alert. Be ready. Be attacking.
BE RELENTLESS.

Let the enemy stop. Let the enemy rest. Let the
enemy finish.
You? Don't finish. Don't stop. Don't rest.
Not until the enemy is completely destroyed.
And even then...Turn your focus inward, on
yourself, and take the opportunity not to rest...
But to make yourself *better, faster,
smarter, stronger.*

Because with those goals,
nothing is ever finished.

APPLICATION

Discipline starts with waking up early.
It really does.
But that is just the beginning;
you absolutely have to apply it to things beyond
waking up early.
It is working out, every day,
making yourself stronger and faster and more
flexible and healthier.
It is eating the right foods,
to fuel your system correctly.
It is disciplining your emotions,
so you can make good decisions.
It is about having the discipline to control your
ego, so it doesn't get out of hand
and control you.
It is about treating people the way you
would want to be treated.
It is about doing the tasks you don't want to
do, but you know will help you.

Discipline is about facing your fears
so you can conquer them.

OF DISCIPLINE

Discipline means taking the hard road—
the uphill road.
    To do what is right.
        For you and for others.
So often, the easy path calls us:
    To be weak for that moment.
        To break down another time.
            To give in to desire and short-term
            gratification.

Discipline will not allow that. Discipline calls
for strength and fortitude and WILL.
It won't accept weakness. It won't tolerate a
breakdown in will.
Discipline can seem like your worst enemy.
    But in reality it is your best friend.
        It will take care of you like nothing
        else can.

And it will put you on the path to strength and
health and intelligence and happiness.
        And most important, discipline will put
        you on the path to FREEDOM.

QUESTIONS

Knowledge is a powerful tool.
It is the master of your tools.
It is where your tools come from, because without
knowledge, there is nothing.
Let's take that one step further: Knowledge is
the ultimate *weapon*; it trumps all other weapons.
Thought is what wins—the MIND is what wins—
knowledge is what wins.
And you gain knowledge by asking questions.
Which questions should you ask?
Simple: Question *everything*. Don't accept
anything as truth.

QUESTION IT ALL.

When you don't understand a word—
get out the dictionary.
When you don't understand a concept—
break it down until you do.
When you don't know how something works—
dig into it until you do.
Ask every question that comes to mind.
That is how you learn.

And most important: Question yourself.
                    Question yourself every day.
Ask yourself:
Who am I? What have I learned? What have I
created? What forward progress have I made? Who
have I helped?
What am I doing to improve myself—today?
     To get better, faster, stronger,
     healthier, smarter?

Is *this* what I want to be? *This?* Is *this* all I've
got—is this everything I can give? Is *this* going
to be *my life?* Do I *accept* that?

Ask yourself those questions, those hard questions
                    and then answer them, truthfully.
And realize that all of us—ALL OF US—can do
better. We can be better.

And it starts when you begin to ask those
questions...
So ask the hard questions of yourself and find
the path to progress and discipline *and to*
freedom inside the answers.

FIGHT

Go down swinging. And I'll tell you:
If you fight with all you have, more often than
not, you won't go down at all. You will win.
But you have to make that attitude a part
of your everyday life.
Do the extra repetition.
Run the extra mile.
Go the extra round.
Make the right choices.

Give the full measure.

Make yourself stronger,
mentally and physically.

Stand and fight.

Fight against weakness. Against fear.
Against time and against decay.
FIGHT BACK.
Go down swinging.
Give every day everything you've got.

And when you face a challenge—even something you
don't believe you can win, or a situation where
you know you cannot win—remember this:
        You have nothing to lose.

So.

STAND UP. GO FORWARD.

Go out in a blaze of glory, fighting with
everything you've got, every ounce of energy,
every bead of sweat, every drop of blood—
until your last breath.

And then—and only then—can you stand down,
put down your sword and your shield, and rest:
in peace.

COMPROMISE

When working with other people and dynamic
situations and relationships and deals, a person,
especially a leader, must compromise.

Finding the common ground between teams.
Merging different approaches to the same problem.
Bridging personalities with people
who might not get along.
Reaching agreements in courses of action.
All of these require compromise.
And in many cases, a failure to compromise is a
failure to succeed.
But those are external compromises, with
other people, other humans that have their
own personalities and ethos and issues. And
compromise is needed to unify.
So to work with them,
compromise is a must.

But internally—it's different.
With myself, I have to hold the line.

There are areas within myself where I CANNOT
compromise.
  I am going to work hard.
    I am going to train hard.
      I am going to improve myself.
        I am not going to rest on my laurels.
          I am going to own my mistakes and
          confront them.
            I am going to face my demons.
              I'm not going to give up, or give
              out, or give in.
                I'm going to stand.

                I am going to maintain
                my self-discipline.

And on those points there will be No Compromise.

NOT NOW.
NOT EVER.

DEFAULT

Proactive and aggressive are similar
and they are both good.
You certainly have to be proactive in the world.
You want to be dictating what happens, not
responding to it.
And yes: That means creating or controlling a
situation as much as you can.

But being aggressive—
that means you are ready to attack.

As I always point out—this doesn't mean you walk
around with your chest puffed out ready to bang
heads with everyone around you.
It doesn't mean you confront people, physically
or mentally, head-on and without a tactically
superior plan.
It doesn't mean you go straight forward into
conflict without thought and without reason.
It doesn't mean you engage in attrition warfare—
no. That is almost never smart.
What it does mean is that you are
going to get after it.

AGGRESSIVE

You are going to move fast.
You are going to think fast.
You are going to outthink and outmaneuver
the enemy.
    If I think the enemy is going to attack
    me—I'm going to attack them first.
    If I think they are going to seize a
    piece of terrain—I am going to be there
    waiting for them.
    If I think the enemy is going to flank
    me—too late—I'm already flanking them.
I don't view aggression as an outward attitude.
I view aggression as an internal character trait.
A fire in your mind that says: I am going to win.
    I am going to battle and I am going to fight
    and I am going to use every tool I have to
    crush my enemy.
    And that tool might be fists,
    but it might be guile.
    It might be a frontal attack,
    but it might be a flanking maneuver.
    It might be an undeniable display of force—
    but it also might be a subtle political maneuver.

And that is what aggression is to me: The unstoppable fighting spirit. The drive. The burning desire to achieve mission success using every possible tool, asset, and strategy and tactic to bring about victory.

IT IS THE WILL. TO. WIN.

And if that kind of internal, relentless aggression is your DEFAULT MODE—

YOU WILL WIN.

NATURE VS. NURTURE

What is more important: Nature or nurture?
In my opinion: Neither.
I have seen people from every stratum of life.
In the military, I worked with
every type of person:
Ivy League kids with silver spoons, former
gangbangers, hood rats, prep school kids, kids from
blue-collar families, kids from strong families and
kids with no families, kids who were pampered and
kids who were abused. And everything in between.
Everything.

And with all those different types of people, there
were good and bad. Successful and unsuccessful.
And in working with businesses, I see the same
thing: People from every walk of life. From the
bottom to the top—and I have seen every type of
person be successful.

So to me, it is not about nature or nurture: It
is about choice.

The people who are successful *decide* they are going to be successful. They make that choice. And they make other choices. They decide to study hard. They decide to work hard. They decide to be the first person to get to work and the last to go home. They decide they are going to take on the hard jobs. Take on the challenges. They decide they are going to lead when no one else will.

They choose who they are going to hang around and they choose who they will emulate.

They choose to become who they want to become—they aren't inhibited by nature or nurture. They overcome both.

And I will tell you something else: It is never too late to make that choice.

You are never too old to decide where you are going to focus your efforts and push to make the most out of every situation.

So. Think not about what you've been through and where you were.

Think about where you are going, and choose.

Choose to make yourself smarter and stronger and healthier.

Choose to work out and study and eat good food and keep your mind clean.

Don't let nature or nurture make you.

Choose to **MAKE. YOUR. SELF.**

FEAR OF

Fear of failure.
Fear of failure can keep you
from taking the risk.
It can leave you sitting there,
paralyzed into not taking action.
And that is obviously bad.
But: I don't want you to overcome fear of
failure.

I want you to be *afraid of failure*.

FEAR OF FAILURE IS GOOD.
Fear of failure will keep you up at night,
planning, rehearsing, going over contingencies.
Fear of failure will keep you training hard.
Fear of failure will stop you from
cutting corners.

Fear of failure will keep you working, thinking,
striving, and relentlessly trying to be more
prepared for battle.
So I want you to be afraid of failing.
I fear failure.

FAILURE

But more important—
I want you to be horrified—
terrified—
of sitting on the sidelines
and doing nothing.

That is what I want you to be afraid of:
Waking up in six days or six weeks or six years
or **SIXTY YEARS** and being no closer to your goal...
You have made **NO PROGRESS**.
That is the horror. That is the nightmare.
That is what you really need to be afraid of:
Being stagnant.

So.

GET UP. AND. GO.

Take the risk, take the gamble, take the first
step. Take action.
And don't let another day
slip
by.

THE WARPATH

The Path.
The Warpath. A Path of War.
The actual definition of "warpath" means moving
toward a battle, a fight—toward war.

And that is what I am doing—and what I have
always been doing.
Whether it was the actual war against our
nation's enemies, or the war against my own
weaknesses—that is what I am doing:

Preparing.
Sharpening my sword.
Honing my skills.

Maintaining the unmitigated daily discipline:
IN ALL THINGS.
And The Warpath is a path—it's a route—
it leads somewhere.
Where does it lead?
Yes, it can lead to war.

And that is fine. Because I am ready; I am waiting.
    But the war might not come. And that is okay.

Because The Warpath is also a war against weakness—
        and so it leads to strength.
It is a war against ignorance—
        and so it leads to knowledge.
It is a war against confusion—
        and so it delivers understanding.
And The Warpath leads to control and to ownership of your life.
That is The Warpath—the path of fire and adversity. The path of blood and sweat and suffering. The Warpath is the interminable path of discipline—
        which is why it leads to **FREEDOM**.

        And beyond that—in the end—The Warpath
        leads: To peace.

SUGARCOATED LIES

Yes, I know.
I know those donuts are tempting.
All those colorful sprinkles.
The cream filling.

The Glaze!
The Glorious Glaze!

And on top of all that: They are free—someone
brought them in and just left them here. Right
here. Right in front of me.
Surely, this must be some kind of sign, some kind
of miracle—right?
I mean: Food is food and if it is free—I pretty
much *need* to eat it.
It would be ungrateful for me to say no.
Right? Right?

WRONG. DEAD WRONG.

Those donuts aren't food.

THEY ARE POISON.

Same with the chocolate chip cookies, the double
Dutch chocolate cake, the can of soda, the bag of
potato chips, and the pretzel-wrapped hot dogs.
All that junk isn't food. It doesn't fuel you. It
kills you. It literally kills you.
It isn't going to make you stronger, faster,
healthier, smarter, or better.
It's going to do the opposite.
And you know this. You know you
DO NOT NEED ANY OF THAT JUNK.
"But it's the only choice."
WRONG.
Unless you have gone an extended period of time
without food, you don't need to eat.
And you definitely don't need to eat that poison.
YOU DON'T NEED TO EAT.
You don't even know what hungry is. Humans can go
thirty days without food.
You can make it.
So. When those foods are tempting you, calling
your name, and enticing you with their **SUGARCOATED
LIES**—get angry. Get aggressive. Stand your ground
in the battle and fight by saying NO.
HOLD THE LINE. Hold the line for your health, your
mental toughness, and to exercise your WILL—
which, I promise, is stronger than the will
of a donut—
if you want it to be.
HOLD THE LINE.

BAD INSTINCTS

There is one instinct to be wary of—
one that you must fight.
This one is a liar.
This one is a saboteur—a backbiter.
And—like the devil himself—he's a
shape-shifter...
He will disguise himself...make you think that he
has got your best interests in mind.
But he doesn't.
This is the instinct that says:

YOU'VE HAD ENOUGH.

You've given it your best shot.
You can stand down.
You can back off.
You can take a knee.
This is the instinct that says: You can rest now.
Do not listen to that instinct.

DO NOT LISTEN.

Because that instinct is a liar
and wants to bring you down.

You see, this instinct is a defense mechanism for your ego.

It gives you an out—a place to run to.

A place of sympathy and amnesty, where all can be forgiven.

Where failures gather together in comfort and drown their sorrows in lies and deception.

They tell each other—and they tell you: "You did the best you could..." and "The deck was stacked against you..." and "It's not your fault..."

And so they tell you: It's okay to stop—it's okay to settle. *IT'S OKAY TO GIVE UP*.

And that is the instinct you need to fight.

To push back—

to smash into the ground.

DO NOT TAKE THE EASY WAY OUT. Do not give up based on instinct. If you are forced to stand down—to retreat so that you can rebuild and re-attack—so be it. But make that decision based on logic—not on the instinct of surrender and defeat. Destroy that instinct.

Replace it with the instinct that says:

GET UP. GO. FIGHT ON.

Make that your fundamental reaction to adversity—MAKE THAT YOUR *GUT* INSTINCT—

and you will overcome anything that stands in your path.

NOT

How do I handle those days when I'm just not
"feeling it"?
Those days when I am tired or worn out or just
sick of the grind...
What do I do on those days?

I GO ANYWAY. I GET IT DONE.

Even if I am just going through the motions—
I GO THROUGH THE MOTIONS.

Don't *really* want to work out? I work out.
Don't *really* want to hammer on a project?
I hammer on the project.
Don't *really* want to get up and get out of bed?
I GET UP AND GET OUT OF BED.
Now—these could be signals that you need some
time off—and those signals might be right.
BUT—don't take today off. Wait until tomorrow.
Don't give in to the immediate gratification that
is whispering in your ear.
SHUT THAT DOWN. DO NOT LISTEN.

FEELING IT

Instead: Go through the motions. Lift the
weights. Sprint the hill. Work on the project.
GET OUT OF BED.
I don't like procrastination. But if you feel
like you need a break—that is one thing you
should procrastinate.
Taking a break is the one thing I put off
until tomorrow.
And if—when tomorrow comes—you still feel like
you need rest or you need a break—then go ahead:
Take it.
Chances are you won't—you won't need that rest.
Chances are you will realize that the desire to
rest was just weakness—it was the desire to take
the path of least resistance—the downhill path—
the downward path.
And by going through the motions, you overcame
that weakness.
And you stayed on the righteous path—the
disciplined path—
        You stayed on The Warpath.

        Right where you know you belong.

REGRET

Regret. The things I could have done differently
or learned sooner. There's so much knowledge
out there, so much information, so many ways to
get better.
And we make so many mistakes.
We are the product of our mistakes.
And oftentimes the lesson is sitting in front of
our face: There to be learned.
But we miss it or we don't pay attention to
it or we think we know better.
Until it punches us in the face.

The most important thing to learn is that
we have so much to learn.

We all do. And we can learn from school and
people and experience and life.
But you have to process the information.
Absorb it. You have to accept it. You have to
open your mind—**FREE YOUR MIND**—so that you can
learn and make real progress.
Are there things I regret and things I wish I
had done differently? Of course. Hindsight is
20/20 and looking back, who wouldn't want to take
another go at something and

improve by doing it again? And then why not do it again, and again, and again?
Who wouldn't want to do things over until you have it perfect?

But the fact is: You don't get that chance. You get one shot.
    We get one shot at this gig right here: Life.
    One life—that's all we've got.
And the most important thing to understand about regret is that in and of itself, regret is worthless. It does nothing for you.
In fact: The only thing valuable in regret is the lesson you learned.
    The knowledge you gained.
But walking around filled with regret gets you nothing.
So. Learn and move on.
Don't let regret beat you down. Don't be a slave to regret.

NO.

Let it teach you. Let it make you better. Let the fear of regret fuel you—to take action—
    today—now.
Take action now to become a person not filled with regret,
    but a person filled with knowledge and
    strength and power
                                    and life.

FOCUS

In combat, focus comes pretty easily because the
battle is right in front of your face.
You have no choice but to focus.
But, sometimes, in day-to-day life,
you can lose track of the long-term goal. It
fades from your vision. It slips from your mind.
WRONG.

I want that long-term goal to be so embedded in
my mind, that I never lose sight of it.
EVER.
And the little tasks and projects and short-
term goals that you tackle need to lead toward
strategic victory—winning the long war.

But we want results **NOW.** We want the shortcut
to the winner's podium.
We need the instant gratification.
And when we don't get the short-term glory,
sometimes we lose sight of those long-term goals.
They *fade.* We lose *focus.*
So we stop the daily tasks and the daily disciplines
that will allow us to achieve our goals. And a day
slips by. And then another day. And a day
turns into a week and a week into a year.
And you look up in six weeks or
six months or six years...

And you've made no progress:

None.

You never moved. In fact: You might be even
further from your goal than you were when you
started. You might have gone backward.
Why? Why did you let that happen?
Because you lost sight of it.
You lost sight of the long-term goal. And it
faded. It faded from memory and the passion dried
up and you began to rationalize:
Maybe I can't. Maybe I don't really want to.
Maybe this goal isn't for me.
And so you give up. You let it go. And you settle.
You settle for the status quo. You settle for the
easy road. You settle for "oh well."

No.

Don't do that. Embed that long-term goal in your
mind. Burn it into your soul.
Think about it, write about it, talk about it.
Hang it up on your wall.
But most important: Do something about it. Every
day. Every day: Do something that moves you
toward that goal—that keeps that goal alive and
in sight and in focus.
However small or insignificant that step might
seem—take it. Do it.
Make it happen. Because that goal isn't going to
achieve itself.

It is All. On. You.

HESITATION

*"Between the acting of a dreadful thing
And the first motion, all the interim is
Like a phantasma or a hideous dream."*

That is Brutus, from Shakespeare's *Julius Caesar*, who, in the play, is plotting to kill Caesar— someone he was loyal to. And Shakespeare—the master of understanding human nature—captures what that feels like. This is how Shakespeare's words would translate today:

"Between the acting of a dreadful thing..."
Between the moment when you are waiting to do something that you don't want to do...
"And the first motion..."
and the moment when you initiate the action...
"All the interim..."
The whole time you are waiting to take that action...
"Is like a phantasma or a hideous dream..." is like an evil spectre, an apparition—a nightmare.

So the battle, the struggle—the hesitation—
takes place in that moment.
That moment, when we must step into the unknown—
that moment filled with fear and horror.
And that fear is what causes hesitation—and
hesitation causes defeat.

HESITATION IS THE ENEMY.

Hesitation allows the moment to pass, the
opportunity to be lost, the enemy to get the
upper hand. Hesitation turns into cowardice.
It stops us from moving forward, from taking
initiative, from executing what we know we must.
Hesitation defeats us. So we must defeat it.

To win, all you have to do is overcome that
moment: The Waiting. The Hesitation. And to do
that, all you have to do is: Go. Move. Take the
action. Get out of bed. Get your feet on the
ground. Step forward.
Do not hesitate.
            Do not wait.
                        Go forward: And win.

DRAW FIRE

Sometimes, bad things happen to good people.
I don't know why. Life is not fair.
That is the reality.
Disease and accidents don't care if their
victim is a "good person."
They have no reason, no justification,
and no mercy.
And even the best person you know can end up in
the clutches of evil.
And you cannot stop it.
So. *What do you do?*
Are you going to get angry? Frustrated?
Are you going to lash out at people?
Who are you going to lash out at?
Are you going to start going down the
spiral of negativity?
Are you going to let the horrible situation dictate
the way you feel and the way you handle it?
Are you going to fall over?
Fall down?
Fall apart?

Or are you going to lead?
Are you going to face this issue with
courage and with resolution?

I say: Lead.

Lead.

Step up. Be the one who people look to.
Absorb the impact—and the negativity.
Draw fire—yes: Draw fire.
That's when a member of a platoon—for tactical
reasons—steps into the open to draw enemy fire;
maybe to give another part of the team a chance
to move; maybe to distract the enemy; maybe to
help the platoon locate the enemy.
But that's what I say: Draw fire. Bring that pain
to me—
        I can handle it when others cannot.
When bad things are happening—I will be the one
good thing—standing tall—that can be relied
upon. I will bolster those around me. And the
positive attitude will spread. And we will fight.
And in fighting, we will win. If not the battle
and if not the war—we will win:
        Because our spirit will never surrender.

And that is the ultimate victory: To hold
your head high, and—even in the face of
inescapable defeat—
        To Stand and Fight.

GOOD

How do I deal with setbacks, failures, delays, defeats, or other disasters? I actually have a fairly simple way of dealing with these situations, summed up in one word: "Good."

This is something that one of my direct subordinates, one of the guys who worked for me, a guy who became one of my best friends, pointed out. He would pull me aside with some major problem or some issue that was going on, and he'd say, "Boss, we've got this thing, this situation, and it's going terribly wrong."

I would look at him and I'd say:"Good."

And finally, one day, he was telling me about something that was going off the rails, and as soon as he finished explaining it to me, he said, "I already know what you're going to say."

And I asked, "What am I going to say?"

And he said, "You're going to say: 'Good.'"

He continued, "That's what you always say. When something is wrong or going bad, you just look at me and say, 'Good.'"

And I said, "Well. I mean it. Because that is

how I operate." So I explained to him that when things are going bad, there's going to be some good that will come from it.

Oh, mission got canceled? Good. We can focus on another one.

Didn't get the new high-speed gear we wanted? Good. We can keep it simple.

Didn't get promoted? Good. More time to get better.

Didn't get funded? Good. We own more of the company.

Didn't get the job you wanted? Good. Go out, gain more experience, and build a better resume.

Got injured? Good. Needed a break from training.

Got tapped out? Good. It's better to tap out in training than to tap out on the street.

Got beat? Good. We learned.

Unexpected problems? Good. We have the opportunity to figure out a solution.

That's it. When things are going bad: Don't get
all bummed out, don't get startled, don't get
frustrated. No. Just look at the issue and say:
"Good."
Now, I don't mean to say something trite; I'm
not trying to sound like Mr. Smiley Positive Guy.
That guy ignores the hard truth. That guy thinks
a positive attitude will solve problems. It
won't. But neither will dwelling on the problem.
No. Accept reality, but focus on the solution.
Take that issue, take that setback, take that
problem, and turn it into something good. Go
forward. And, if you are part of a team, that
attitude will spread throughout.
Finally: if you can say the word "good," then
guess what?
It means you're still alive.
It means you're still breathing.
And if you're still breathing, that means you've
still got some fight left in you.
So get up, dust off,
reload, recalibrate, re-engage—
and go out on the attack.

DEATH

But how does "good" apply to the worst of losses:
the death of a loved one? It is easy to think that
there is nothing "good" in death.
But then I remember the people I have lost
throughout my life: the memories of them, the
experiences, the fun, their unique personalities, and
everything they gave me. Not only in their
life, but in their death.
What their life taught me,
and what their death taught me.
The mark they have left on me.
And I realized, there is good; even in death
there is good.
First of all, I was lucky to have had that person in
my life; even if it was only for a short time—too
short a time—at least I got that. Those
precious moments, those unforgettable memories,
at least I got those and got to experience those
times—to know the beauty of their personality,
their attitude, their outlook on the world.
They were all unique, and I am thankful for the
opportunity I had to interact with them.
Now, comes death.
Death is horrible and death is wretched and
death is cruel. And: Death isn't fair.

And I don't know why the best people seem to be
taken from us first.
Death is also inescapable. There is no way out.
No one gets out alive.
Death is part of life, like the contrast between
the darkness and the light.
                    Without death, there is no life.
And the people that I have lost: They taught me that.
They taught me how precious life is.
How blessed we are to have every day. *To learn.*
To grow. To laugh. To live.

To Live.

To live every day with purpose and passion.
To wake up in the morning and be thankful—
thankful for that morning— thankful for that
opportunity to go into the world and live.

Live for them. For those who don't have the opportunity.
          For those who were stolen away by
          death's cruel hand.
For them, I will live. I will revere their memory
and I will live.

So. Let us cry no more. Let us mourn no more.
Let us remember—but let us not dwell...
Instead: Let us laugh and love and let us embrace
and venerate everything that life is and every
opportunity it gives us.
Let us *LIVE*—for those WHO live no more.
                    Let us live to honor them.

EVERY

This isn't a part-time gig.
This isn't punch the clock and go home for the day.
You don't get weekends off.

No.

Here: There's no such thing as a weekend.
This is an everyday gig: Every day is a Monday.
And you might not like that.

Me? I love it.
To me, every day is a beginning.
A new day.

A new week.

A new shot at life.

An opportunity to come out of the gate like a man
possessed and attack the day:

DAY

Without mercy.

Today: I'm taking scalps.

> I'm putting the pressure on.
>> *I'm the aggressor.*
>>> *I'm on the attack.*

And of course: I will get tired.
> I will get beat up.
>> I will get knocked down and drained
and will have some bad days.
But I
> *will*

not

> **Stop.**

NO ◊

No more.
No more.

NO MORE.

No more excuses.
No more: "I'll start tomorrow."
No more: "Just this once."
No more accepting the shortfalls of my own will.
No more taking the easy road.
No more bowing down to whatever unhealthy or
unproductive thoughts
float through my mind.

No.

No more.
No more waiting for the perfect moment
and no more indecision
and no more lies.
No more weakness.

MORE

No.

No more.

Now is the time for strength.

And through strength—
       and through will—
            and through unwavering discipline—

I will become *what* I want to be.
I will become *who* I want to be.
And then—and only then—will I rest and say:

                  No more.

STAYING

Don't worry about motivation.
Motivation is fickle. It comes and goes.
It is unreliable and when you are counting on
motivation to get your goals accomplished—you
will likely fall short.
So.
Don't expect to be motivated every day to get out
there and make things happen. You won't be.
Don't count on motivation.
Count on Discipline.

You know what you have to do.
So:

MAKE YOURSELF DO IT.

You do that with Discipline.

MOTIVATED

Everyone wants some magic pill—some life hack—
that eliminates the need to do the work.
But that does not exist.
No.

    You have to do the work.
        You've got to hold the line.
            You've got to MAKE IT HAPPEN.
So.
    Dig in.
        Find the Discipline.
            Be the Discipline.
ACCOMPLISH.

                                    That's it.

ME VERSUS ME

There are people in the world who have skills
and strength and talent that I will never have.
Never.
These notions that you can "be whatever you want
to be as long as you want it bad enough" are not
true. They are fairy tales.
We all have limitations. I don't have the right
genes to be an Olympic weightlifter. I don't have
the right genetics to be an Olympic sprinter.
Or gymnast. Sure, if I trained my whole life,
perhaps I could have become fairly decent in
those sports.
But the best in the world? No. I simply do not
have the DNA to be the best in the world
in those categories.
But what does that mean?
Does that mean I give up? Does that mean I quit?
Of course not. Not at all.
It means that I am going to try to be
the best that I can be.
The strongest.
The fastest.
The smartest human being that I can become.

That is what I am going to go for. And it doesn't
matter that I will not be better than others
when I compare myself to them. No, I will look at
others who do achieve greatness in a category,
and I will say:
      Look at what is possible.
          How close can I get to that greatness?
           How close can I get to that glory?
But my glory, it doesn't happen in front of a crowd.
      It doesn't happen in a stadium or on a stage.
      There are no medals handed out.
It happens in the darkness of the early morning.

In solitude.

Where I try. And I try. And I try again.
With everything I have, to be the best that I can
possibly be.
      Better than I was yesterday.
         Better than people thought I could be.
         Better than I thought I could be.
Faster and stronger and smarter.
And claim one victory that no one can ever take
away from me. Ever.
      A victory that is earned every single day.
         A victory of determination and will and
         discipline.
         A victory achieved because:
         I will not stop.

REMAIN

It wasn't in a war.
It wasn't in a battle.
It isn't in a melee of fire and destruction that
most of us succumb to weakness.
We are taken apart, slowly.
Convinced to take an easier path.
Enticed by comfort.
Most of us aren't defeated in one decisive battle.
We are defeated one tiny, seemingly insignificant
surrender at a time that chips away at who we
should really be.
It isn't that you wake up one day and decide
that's it: I am going to be weak.
No. It is a slow incremental process.
It chips away at our will—it chips
away at our discipline.
We sleep in a little later.
We miss a workout, then another.
We start to eat what we shouldn't eat
and drink what we shouldn't drink.

VIGILANT

And, without realizing it—one day, you wake
up and you have become something that you never
would have allowed.
Instead of strong—you are weak.
Instead of disciplined—you are disorganized
and lost.
Instead of moving forward and progressing—you
are moving backward and decaying.
And those things happen without you seeing them.
              Without you recognizing them.

So.

You *have to* **BE VIGILANT**. You have to be **ON GUARD**.
You *have to* **HOLD THE LINE** on the seemingly
insignificant little things—
      things that shouldn't matter—but that **do**.

FEAR

Fear is normal.
Every person feels fear at some point.
What should you do?
Step.
Step.
Take the step.

Step aggressively toward your fear—that is the
step into bravery.

We are scared of what we don't know, and there is
but one way to confront that fear:

Step. GO.

And that simple action, this simple attitude
answers so many questions.
How do you get to the gym every day?

Step. GO.

How do you change your diet?
          Step. GO.

How do you overcome fear of failure or fear of
success or fear of fear itself?
          Step. GO.

How do you face the fear of the unknown?
          Step. GO.

Don't wait anymore.
     Don't think anymore.
          Don't plan anymore.
               Don't contemplate anymore.
Don't make any more excuses or justifications.
               Don't rationalize anything else.

No. No. **NO. NO.**

Instead: Be aggressive.
          Take action.
                    Now.
And the first action you need to take?
          The first step you need to take?
The first step you need to take is just that:
Step.
          Step.
               Go.
                    Now.

THE DARKNESS

The sun doesn't shine every day.
The storms will come.
There are times when the nights will be long and
dark and you will be alone.
There will be times when The Darkness seems to
consume everything.

But don't let it consume you.

Don't let it *consume* you.

Even in the darkest times.
Even in the strongest storms.
Even when the sun is blotted out
and the world is falling apart.

The Darkness cannot extinguish your light.

You.

Your WILL. Your determination.

No matter what is happening—no matter how hard
the fight is.

As long as you keep fighting—you win.

Only surrender is defeat.

Only quitting is the end.

Because The Darkness only wins if you let it.

> Do not let The Darkness win.
>
> Fight.
>
> Fight on.
>
> To fight against The
> Darkness is to win.
>
> **Fight on.**

OVERWHELMED

Yes. Life can be overwhelming.
That's the way life works. It is testing you.
It is going to throw problems at you and it is
going to throw them at you all at the same time.
This is the way life works: Murphy's Law.
It is easy to feel beaten when you are faced with
all those problems at once.
But let me tell you, that does not mean
give up fighting.
In fact: It means the opposite.
It is time for you to fight harder.

To dig in.
To go on The Warpath.

To assess what the problems are, and decide
which one you are going to attack first.
Then, get started.

Attack.

And listen: It won't be easy.
In fact: It will be hard.

Life is hard.
        That's what *life* is.
And these challenges you face, they are going to
do their best to
Take
        you
                down.

DO NOT LET THEM.

Stand up. *Dig in.*
    Line up those problems and confront them—
    face them—fight them.

DO NOT LET THEM BRING YOU DOWN.

Instead, let these challenges raise you up—let
them elevate you.
Let their demands and their trials make you
stronger—let the adversity you face today turn
you into a better person tomorrow.
So in the future, you look back at these
struggles and you say to them:
    Thank you—
            you made me better.

NEGATIVE TALK

The old classic. What do you do about the negative person talking behind your back and trying to bring you down?
Sure you can *confront* them and join them in their little game.
You can give them the satisfaction of knowing that they got *in your head*.
You can turn your life into a grade school gossip hall.
Of course, there are times, unfortunately, that you have to engage with people like this. You may have to set the record straight on a serious allegation. You may have to challenge statements that might be damaging to the team or the mission.
And when you do have to engage, do it professionally. Say something like:

"I heard you had some pointers for me about how I'm doing my job. I'd love to get your feedback so I can tighten up my game."

FROM NEGATIVE PEOPLE

A statement like that will likely diffuse the scenario. The person will know that there are informants who will tell you what is going on. And that will likely stifle the situation. But let me tell you what my preferred methodology is for this situation:

It is simple:

Ignore and outperform.

Yes. While you are over there watching me and talking about me—*I'm working.*
I'm working hard. I'm taking things to the next level.
You keep gossiping—*I'll keep working.*
You keep talking smack—*I'll keep working.*
You keep chattering about things—*I'll keep working.*
You keep focusing on what everyone else is doing

wrong—*I'll keep focusing* on what I can do RIGHT.
And when you finally look around at where you are
and where I am
—you will realize that you have nothing
to talk smack about.

Because you will lose.
And I. Will. Win.

And this applies to when people are playing
office politics or forming their cliques or
working their personal agendas.
Of course—sometimes you have to
play those games too.
But when dealing with people like this,
let your first course of action and the
fundamental core of how you handle it be very
clear and very direct:

Outwork and **outperform** every last one of them.

HOLD THE LINE

Instead of going backward—instead of decaying—get stronger.

Get better.

Grow and learn and develop—and live.

Live in defiance of the weakness and in rebellion against the decay.

Fight them as they creep in with their offers of instant gratification and immediate rewards.

Fight them for every inch they try to take.

Do not surrender any ground.

EVER.

BEGIN

This is where it begins.

In the darkness.

Before the sun and the birds and the world.

Every day.

When the alarm sounds.

IT IS TIME.

Rise.
Despite fatigue and soreness.

Curse the warmth of the bed.
Curse the comfort of the pillow.
Fight the temptation of weakness.

Get up and go.

Do it quickly, without thought.
Do not reason with weakness. You cannot.

You must only take action.

Get up

and GO.

ENGAGE

Engage.

Weakness is strong.
I must be *stronger*.

I must crush it into submission.
Through force of will.

So. I savage the body.
I push and pull and fight against gravity.

I fight against fatigue and soreness and the
weakness that says:

> Give in.
>
> I will not give in.
>
> I will fight.

LAUGHTER

Sure there is darkness everywhere.
And I have seen my share.
But that is not where I live my life.
At all.
In fact, the opposite is true.
I am not wandering around, suffering in despair.

No.

I am having fun.

FUN.

I am laughing.
I am joking.
I am clowning around making fun of
everything and everyone.
Especially of myself.
I'm an easy target to poke fun at.
And I'm good with that.

WINS

Because, sure: Life is tough.
But it gets a lot easier when you are laughing at it.

So.

Despite the suffering.
In fact:
To spite the suffering.
    To spite the hardships.
       To spite the challenges.
Laugh at them all.

They can't stand it when you do.
And they all get easier.
Yes: Laugh at them all.

Laughter wins.

PART 2:

ACTIONS

PHYSICAL TRAINING: GETTING AFTER IT

PHYSICAL

There are all kinds of benefits
from physical training.
You will be healthier.
This is a fact.
By working out, you will increase your
endorphins, testosterone, growth hormones,
cardiac volume, insulin sensitivity,
and natural killer cells.
Those changes will help prevent or treat the
following health issues: high blood pressure,
obesity, heart disease, type 2 diabetes,
insomnia, and depression.

BOOM.

Still not convinced?
Working out will make you smarter. Yes: *Smarter*.
It improves blood flow to the brain.
It boosts growth hormones
that promote growth of new nerve cells.

TRAINING

It improves synaptic plasticity, the ability for neurons to send and receive messages.
It releases brain chemicals that help cognition, like: dopamine, glutamate, norepinephrine, and serotonin.
It also boosts the production of brain-derived neurotrophic factor (BDNF), a protein that helps with mental processes.

But, don't just take my word for it.
        Go. Do.
Get some exercise done and pay attention to your mental state. You will feel more aware, sharper, and smarter.

THIS IS REAL.

STRESS:

Stress is good and bad.
In order to improve, we need stress. We need
to push the body and the mind in order to get
better.
One of our main physical reactions to stress is
the release of the hormone cortisol into the
body. It has a multitude of effects, including
making glucose available to the brain, generating
energy from stored reserves, and focusing energy
on immediate threats rather than less urgent
needs. It also raises blood pressure to optimize
the flow of blood throughout the body.

But, stress can also be bad. If we are under
too much stress, and cortisol is released into
the body too often, it begins to have negative
effects, like a car running "in the red" for
extended periods of time. When cortisol levels
remain consistently high, the immune system can
become repressed, increasing blood pressure and
causing hypertension—a sustained high blood
pressure that causes damage to the heart and

GOOD AND BAD

blood vessels. It can also encourage fat deposits and even cause some level of bone loss.

Exercise is a form of stress and does cause the release of cortisol. However, just as exercise conditions the muscles and the heart, it also conditions the body to react properly to the release of cortisol and trains the body to keep cortisol levels balanced. Excessive regular release of cortisol can also be a significant factor in overtraining—when we push the body too hard, excessive cortisol leads to fatigue and a drop in performance.

So you have to be careful not to stress the body and mind too much. But again: **YOU MUST STRESS THE BODY AND MIND SOME IN ORDER TO IMPROVE.**

WHEN?

The biggest excuse not to work out is lack of time.

Something always comes up.

But there is one time of day that no can take away from you: predawn.

The military has a term: "Stand To." It means get up early and be ready for enemy attack. It has been a standard practice for many wars. For instance, in World War One, each man was expected to be awake well before first light, standing on the trench fire step, rifle loaded, bayonet fixed, and ready to repel an attack.

Further back in history, from Rogers' Rangers Standing Orders: "All hands shall be awake, alert and ready for action before dawn. Dawn's when the French and Indians like to attack."

So.
Get up before the sun. Be ready to
                                        attack.

Yes, that means

                    GET UP EARLY!

This will be hard at first, but it will
become normal.

And once you are accustomed to it,
early rising is guaranteed to make
your day better.

                    So **GET AFTER IT.**

PSYCHOLOGICAL

There are a slew of psychological advantages that come from early morning physical training. First, there is a psychological win over the enemy. Knowing that you are working harder than your adversaries gives you an advantage. It gives you confidence that you can overcome them in battle.

Another advantage to waking up early and working out hard is that it demands discipline to do both. Now, some scientists have claimed that discipline dissipates the more it is used—that willpower is a finite resource that is reduced every time it is used during the day.

This is wrong. That does *not happen*.

To the contrary, I believe, and studies have shown, that discipline and willpower do not go down as they are called into action—they actually get stronger.

EDGE

This is obvious if you actually try the experiment yourself:
Before you go to bed, plan what workout you are going to do in the morning. Stage your workout clothes so you don't even have to think when you get up. Write down a list of things you need to accomplish the next day. Set your alarm clock for 4:30 a.m. and go to sleep.

When the alarm clock goes off—get up. Put on your pre-staged clothes. Brush your teeth and go get your workout on. Hard. Get done, shower, get dressed, and begin to crush your list of tasks for the day.

When it is time for breakfast, see what happens. You won't want to eat junk. You won't want that disgusting donut. You will want some eggs and bacon. And that will happen at lunch too. You are feeling good. Energized. You don't want to eat the worthless calories of pizza or French fries. You want fuel. Good fuel to rebuild your body. Clean fuel that keeps your mind sharp. When you are on the path you want to stay on the path.

Unfortunately, the opposite is also true. Once you step off the path, you tend to stray far. When you don't prepare what you need to do the next day, when you sleep in and then skip your workout and you don't start attacking the tasks you have—because you didn't write them down the night before—that is when you make bad decisions. That is when your will and discipline fail. You figure you might as well have that donut for breakfast and once you have done that, might as well put down four or five pieces of pizza for lunch. *It doesn't matter anymore*—you're off the path and that is a disaster. Your will didn't break—it never showed up in the first place.

So. Get on the path of discipline and stay on the path.

Discipline begets discipline.
Will propagates **MORE WILL**.

Hold the line across the line and victory will be yours.

SLEEP

Sleep is a necessity. Humans need sleep. Failure to get enough sleep has serious side effects. Lack of sleep can cause negative hormonal changes, interfere with the metabolizing of glucose, increase blood pressure, and suppress the immune system. Less sleep also means less human growth hormone in your body, which means less muscle mass and weaker bones. Mentally, the brain is impacted as the ability to pay attention and concentrate begins to diminish and problem solving and basic reasoning become less acute. Furthermore, over an extended period, there are psychological effects like paranoia and even hallucinations.

But how much sleep is enough? Different people need different amounts of sleep. Newborns can sleep up to seventeen hours a day; toddlers can sleep up to twelve hours a day. As people grow older, less sleep is required. Teens generally need eight to ten hours and by the time people are full adults eight hours

becomes the standard—though the actual number
is between seven and nine hours, depending on
the individual. Some people genetically need even
less sleep than that, but those people are rare.
I am one of those people.

But it isn't only genetics.

You can also sleep less and fall asleep faster if
you are in good physical condition, eating clean,
and have a clear mind.

For me, the better the condition I'm in and the
cleaner I eat, the more quickly I will fall asleep,
and the less sleep I need.

So, while I do have short-sleep genetics on my
side, equally important is that I stay healthy
and eat clean.

And finally, I choose not to sleep in.
I don't give in to the temptation of the warm
blankets and soft pillow.

> I mobilize the will to get me out of
> bed and into the game.

Obviously, I am an advocate of waking up early.
But, since sleep must be a priority to maintain

health, how can we get enough sleep and still wake up early?
The answer is simple:

Go to bed earlier.

Going to bed at 10 p.m. and waking up at 5 a.m. gets you a solid seven hours.

Go to bed at 9:55 p.m. and you can get up at 4:55 a.m., still get your seven hours, and be up before the enemy.

Try it. If you get up and get out of bed at 4:55, a vast majority of the world is still sleeping.

You aren't.
You are up getting after it.

The world is yours when you are up before the enemy.

There is no traffic. The gym is empty. There is no one to distract you or call you or send you some stupid text about something you don't care about.

It's just you.

So, go to bed early, and wake up early.
People constantly ask me for the secret of
getting up early.
I tell them it is simple:

SET YOUR ALARM CLOCK AND
GET OUT OF BED WHEN IT GOES OFF.

That's it.
Is it easy? No.
Everyone likes that warm bed.
Everyone needs just five more minutes of slumber
in the morning.
So they hit snooze. They roll over.
They go back to sleep.

No.

Get up and get going. And one thing that will
help you do that is going to bed earlier, which
can be at least as hard, if not harder, than
waking up.

FALLING

Yes. It can be just as hard for some people to go to sleep early as it is to wake up—if not harder.

So here are some steps to help that:

1. GET TIRED. Yes, get tired. If you are not active throughout the day, you won't be tired. Getting a hard workout in the early morning will not only energize you during the day but will also make you fall asleep faster at night. Getting a morning workout and another workout at lunch or after work will also get you tired. Unfortunately, you may find that working out just prior to going to bed will keep you awake, so try not to work out any closer than two hours before you want to sleep.

2. Turn off the computer. Turn off the smartphone. Stop checking social media and stop watching *one more* YouTube video. Sure, there is some science that says that the light from computer and phone screens tricks your mind

ASLEEP

into thinking it is daylight and time to get
up. But on top of that, the internet is filled
with professionals that create content with the
sole purpose of getting you to click on it. Yes,
clickbait is real, and just like a bait used
in fishing, it is a trick to get you hooked.
So: Don't. Don't click it. You will get nothing
positive from it. **AT ALL.**

3. Read. If your mind is still active when you
reach your bedtime—that's okay. Get into bed
and get a book and start reading. Reading is
relaxing. It settles your mind. And it makes
you smarter. So do it. And if the book you are
reading is *too good* and makes you want to stay up
and read—simple—don't read that book. Read a
boring one—an educational one—but a boring one.
That will send you to sleep.

4. Most important: The key to getting to sleep
early is GETTING UP EARLY. No, it might not help
you *tonight* but tomorrow night it will. If you

need seven full hours of sleep, and you want to get up at 4:30 a.m., that means you need to go to bed at 9:30 p.m. But it can be hard to force yourself to sleep at 9:30. So. You stay up until 11:30. You should STILL GET UP AT 4:30. Yes, that will be only five hours of sleep. And yes, you will likely feel tired through the day—which is actually good, because at the end of the day, you WANT TO BE TIRED. Now, you *can* go to bed at 9:30—you are now on track.

5. Do it every day. People ask me if I still get up early on the weekends. YES. For a bunch of reasons. Obviously, the weekend is only two days so I want to get up and take advantage of it. I get up early, get my workout done, and complete any must-do tasks as quickly as possible. That allows for time to relax and enjoy without things hanging over your head. The other reason I wake up early on weekends is to keep my sleep pattern consistent. If I sleep in to 5:30 or 6 a.m. on Saturday, I will likely stay awake a couple of

extra hours on Saturday night, which now has me sleeping in until 7 a.m. on Sunday, which now has me awake even later on Sunday night—which means when I go back to waking up at 4:30 on Monday, I haven't gotten the sleep I need. So: Don't break the cycle. Get up early every day. If you need extra sleep, take a power nap.

POWER NAPS

Power naps. They are real. If you are feeling
tired they can be a lifesaver. And if you are
feeling tired due to lack of sleep, they can be
very powerful. I have a technique for power naps
that is a combination of two things I learned.

The first was in high school. My anatomy and
physiology teacher was a high-energy, passionate
teacher. But if you went into his classroom
during lunch, you would find him sitting in a
chair with his feet elevated on the lab tables,
sleeping. He did it just about every day. One day
I asked him about it; he said his goal was to
elevate his feet above his heart and sleep for
ten to fifteen minutes before he ate his lunch.
He said the nap gave him energy. Elevating his
feet above his heart took the strain off the
circulatory system in his lower body and helped
move some of the blood that might have pooled in
his feet and legs. I began to try it occasionally
and it certainly felt good.

But I really noticed it when I got to BUD/S, the basic SEAL training course. Obviously, we were operating in a fairly sleep-deprived environment there on an almost daily basis and the schedule was very tight, going from evolution to evolution throughout the day, on a strict timeline. But there were some holes in the schedule, usually ten to fifteen minutes a couple of times a day for us to prepare for our next evolution and use the bathroom. During those breaks, if I got the chance, I would lie down on the floor, put my feet up on my bed, set my alarm for six to eight minutes, and sleep. Of course, I was tired, so I would fall asleep very quickly, and when the alarm would go off, I would wake up and feel completely refreshed. It was awesome.

When I got to the SEAL Teams, I used the same technique and found it especially helpful during long patrols in the field. When we formed a perimeter for a break and I wasn't on security, I would immediately elevate my feet and take a power nap. The effects were even more obvious, since on a patrol we were on our feet for many hours carrying a heavy load.

I still use this effective technique when I am overly tired.

Warning: Be careful about letting your six- to eight-minute nap turn into a two-hour slumber. If you do this, you will have trouble falling asleep at night, which leads to trouble waking up in the morning. That means there is a higher chance you will fall off the early morning schedule.

THE WORKOUTS

Everyone wants to know: What should a workout actually consist of?

And first of all—let me say this: The most important thing to do is
SOMETHING.
ANYTHING.

Walk. Jog. Calisthenics. Swim. Lift some weights. Hike. Stretch. Do burpees. Play a game of basketball or go get on the jiu-jitsu mat. Some people aren't sure what to do for a workout—but that is often just an excuse.

Exercise doesn't need to be some complex, multi-level, multi-dimensional, scientifically proven methodology. But it does need to be SOMETHING.

Once you begin doing something, it is a good idea to track it. Recording weights, repetitions, and times is useful. The records allow you to track progress. They can serve as goals. They also let you know when you are overtraining. But, it is important to pay attention to your state at the end of a workout. The more experienced you become at working out, the easier this is. You will know when to push. You will know that there are days to hold back.

My workouts are divided into some broad types of movements: Pull, Push, Lift, Squat. In addition to those, the workouts focus working the "Gut" and metabolic conditioning (MetCon).

For the purposes of this field manual, I have established three basic levels of exercises: Beginner, Intermediate, Advanced.

This is only a guide. As you become stronger, more experienced, and more in tune with your body and your desired outcomes, make adjustments. Read and learn. Try new systems. Learn new exercises. Try new movements and new sports. Mix it up and have fun. Push yourself, but do so in a measured way so you avoid burnout, overtraining, and injury.

To see the actual workouts, go to

Appendix: The Workouts

Again, use the workouts as a guide. Learn about your own body. Push yourself. Most important: Be consistent. And consistency starts with GETTING IN THE GYM. If you are tired or sore or burned out, don't just give up completely. Go to the gym and stretch. Move. Do some light exercises. But keep the routine in place.

Too often, people take the day off. And that turns into two. And two into three. And then they have gone a week without getting in a good workout.
SO.
    Maintain the routine.
    Maintain the discipline.

BUILDING THE

Having a gym in your home eliminates all kinds of excuses. There is nothing more convenient than having your gym collocated with your domicile. I have had a garage gym since I have had a garage. But garage gyms don't need to be in a garage— they can go anywhere: basements, spare bedrooms, offices, backyards, front yards, patios, car-ports...anywhere. Just like anything else in life, you do what you can with what you've got.

Once you have carved out some space, it is time to start getting equipment in place. Start with a pull-up bar. You can mount one just about anywhere and once you have a pull-up bar, you can work your whole body with all the varieties of pull-ups, push-ups, gut work, and squats.

Another useful and relatively cheap piece of equipment is gymnastic rings. They can also be mounted just about anywhere and allow a great number of exercises, including: ring dips, ring pull-ups, ring push-ups, L-sits, all kinds of various holds, and countless variants of each of those.

HOME GYM

Next up is a squat rack, which should include a pull-up bar and some kind of dip bar attachment. With the squat rack, a barbell and weights are needed. Rubber bumper plates allow for dynamic lifts like the clean and jerk and the snatch.

That's it. That's all you need.

That basic setup should go a long way in achieving exceptional fitness. Beyond that there are countless implements to include in your arsenal when time and budget allow. Kettlebells are probably the next addition, then a rowing machine and/or an air bike. A Glute-Ham Developer (GHD) is another piece of equipment that is definitely nice to have at home. Medicine balls, plyometric boxes, bands, chains, club bells, sledgehammers are also fun to use. But, while all those pieces of equipment are nice to have and can add some variety to training, none of them are really necessary, and although I have all those in my gym, I still most consistently use the basic equipment: pull-up bar, dip bars, rings, squat rack, and barbell with bumper plates.

MARTIAL

Everyone should train in martial arts,
just as everyone should eat.

But just as food is different and varies greatly
in how it affects your body, not all martial arts
are created equal.

There are three broad forms of martial arts:
grappling, striking, and weapons.

Grappling uses leverage and holds to control or
submit your opponent. Striking uses punches,
kicks, knees, elbows, headbutts, and any other
body parts to hit the opponent. Martial arts with
weapons obviously utilize a variety of weapons,
including sticks, knives, and, in the modern
world, firearms.

Perhaps the most critical form of self-defense is
the mind. By being smart and aware, you can avoid
situations that are likely to expose you

ARTS

to danger. That being said, there are times when your mind and your intelligence can no longer help you. That is the reality. In those cases, the ultimate form of self-defense is obviously the firearm. It is an equalizer without parallel and is simply unmatched in its ability to eliminate an attacker regardless of size and strength. If a person truly needs self-protection in a high-threat area, there is no substitute for the firearm. Even in an area that might be considered low-threat, there are no guarantees. There have been horrific home invasions, carjackings, kidnappings, and other vicious and violent attacks in some of the most prestigious neighborhoods in the world that were also considered to be the safest. There is no choice but to be prepared.

Of course, mishandled firearms are extremely dangerous and can cause serious injury and death to the owner or other innocent people if they are not handled with the four principles of firearm safety constantly in mind:

1. Treat every gun as if it is loaded.
2. Never point your gun at something you are not willing to destroy.
3. Keep your finger off the trigger until your sights are on target.
4. Always be sure of your target and what is behind it.

Additionally, firearms should always be stored in a safe place where they cannot fall into the wrong hands.

Most important, without proper training, possessing a firearm is useless, or even more dangerous to its owner than not having one. Learning how to shoot quickly and accurately while under stress is absolutely mandatory if one is going to own a firearm. This means finding a good instructor at a quality range to participate in firearms training.

Safety is paramount in firearms training. When treated properly and with respect, firearms training is safe. Not only does it prepare you for worst-case-scenario confrontations, but also provides additional benefits even if you never need to utilize your firearm for self-protection.

Firearms training builds hand-eye coordination, speed, concentration, and instincts. It demands repetitive movement to develop muscle memory and demands a high level of proprioception when shooting in a dynamic situation. Finally, training competitively for speed and accuracy conditions you for high-pressure situations by teaching the need to relax, detach, get control of breathing, and focus on the immediate task at hand.

● ● ●

But firearms are not always available. There are many places in the world where carrying a gun is illegal. There are also times where firearms malfunction. So it is important to know how to defend yourself in unarmed situations, which brings us back to martial arts.

First let me say that the martial arts are very emotional for some people. Their martial art becomes their religion and they become blinded by it. Martial arts are not static. They evolve all the time. If you do not evolve with them, you will be left behind. Picking one martial art versus another or saying that one martial art is "better" than another martial art drives some people crazy. I do not engage in irrational theoretical discussions on which martial art is best. There is no reason to theorize anymore.

The Ultimate Fighting Championship (UFC) put many theories to the test. The wars in Iraq and Afghanistan also put many theories about hand-to-hand combat to the test. Finally, every person now carries a video camera in their pocket and there are thousands of street fights and confrontations to watch on the internet.

With all that information readily available, there is no need to theorize anymore. It is easy to see what works and what doesn't. Furthermore, it is also obvious that martial arts are not stagnant. They evolve. People develop new techniques and new moves to counter other techniques and other moves. But the fundamental principles do not change—they only become reinforced.

With all this information available and with so many theories now tested in the cage, on the street, and in combat, martial arts are no longer just a theory. There is simple, pragmatic reality.

So, here are my recommendations on which martial arts to learn and how to proceed down the path of learning martial arts.

Start with Brazilian jiu-jitsu. It is a form of grappling that is highly advanced because, for the most part, the actual fighting takes place on the ground. This is a key point, because our first form of self-defense is to get away—yes, run. If you are confronted by another person or a group of people, the best thing you can do is run away: avoid the conflict. This is relatively easy if someone is trying to strike you with punches or kicks. They do not have control over you, so you can simply run away from them. You have won.

The problem comes in a self-defense situation when someone is grabbing you. Now they are preventing your first line of defense: Running away. As soon as someone grabs you, you are in a grappling scenario, and one of the most critical parts of Brazilian jiu-jitsu is escaping from someone's grip so you can run.

Oftentimes, an attacker will take you to the ground in order to prevent you from escaping their grip. When this happens, the ability to ground fight is used not to stay on the ground but to get up and get away from the attacker. The first goal of a beginner in jiu-jitsu is not to get the fight to the ground, but to get up off the ground and get away. This is an important distinction from people who believe the goal of self-defense in jiu-jitsu is to get the attacker to the ground. This is not true. The goal is to get away. But, as has been seen over and over again, fights often end up on the ground, and therefore a person must be prepared for it. Not training in jiu-jitsu because you don't want to go to the ground is like not learning to swim because you don't want to go in the water. It doesn't make sense. The safest way to deal with water is to be comfortable in it—just as being comfortable on the ground is the best way to deal with that scenario, should it unfold in real life.

• • •

Another reason I recommend starting martial arts by learning Brazilian jiu-jitsu is because it is the most complex of the martial arts. Although there is a finite number of basic moves and positions, there is an infinite number of moves beyond the basics, and more are developed every day in this constantly evolving art. Due to this unending depth in jiu-jitsu, it is also the most cerebral of the martial arts. It provides incredible mental stimulus and a never-ending challenge to learn, develop, and improve. Jiu-jitsu never gets old.

The next martial art I recommend learning is boxing. Boxing is an incredibly effective striking art despite its relative simplicity: There are only two weapons in boxing—the left hand and the right hand. But with those two weapons, an incredible advantage can be gained if you know how to throw them in effective combinations. Other critical elements learned in boxing are angles, movement (both of which are based heavily on footwork), and speed, which are utilized in both the offense and defense of boxing. With basic boxing knowledge, a person can throw effective punches and avoid being punched— both extremely useful assets when attempting the primary goal of self-defense: Run. Boxing develops the ability to hit quickly, avoid being hit, and run away from the area of confrontation.

The next two martial arts to invest time into are Muay Thai and wrestling. They both add a plethora of options and skills to any fighter.

Muay Thai adds a massive arsenal of striking options to a fighter. Where boxing utilizes only the fists, Muay Thai utilizes the fists, the elbows, the knees, and the shins in very aggressive combinations that are absolutely devastating in a fight. Muay Thai is also about pain and the ability to withstand pain.

The conditioning of the shins to kick and shield kicks, as well as the conditioning of the body and legs to absorb punishment, is brutal and requires an iron will. Muay Thai also offers great work in striking from the clinch position, when an opponent is grabbing you by the head and/or arms. The strikes from this close range, especially the knees and elbows, are vicious. Techniques are also taught to trip or sweep the opponent to the ground that are powerful and effective.

Wrestling is a grappling art, perhaps the most widely known and practiced. It is an amazing sport for conditioning of both the mind and the body. The physical grind of wrestling hardens the body and mind without mercy. On top of the conditioning and mental toughness derived from wrestling, it is also king of position in martial arts—meaning a good wrestler can decide what position they will be in during a confrontation. No other martial art provides the practitioner a better ability to dictate the position of a fight with one simple idea: The main focus of wrestling is to get an opponent to the ground and keep them there. This means wrestling increases the ability not only to take an adversary to the ground and keep them there, but also the ability to defend yourself from being taken to the ground. So, if you are more skilled in wrestling than your opponent, you can dictate where you fight. If you are a better striker than your opponent, you can defend their takedown and win the fight on your feet. If your opponent is a better striker, you can take them to the ground and defeat them with superior grappling. Unfortunately, submission holds do not exist in wrestling, so there are no techniques taught on how to actually finish fights. That being said, there are some practitioners of what is known as "catch wrestling" who continue to teach extremely effective submission holds that were outlawed by the sport as wrestling gained popularity.

. . .

Once a good base is established in Brazilian jiu-jitsu, boxing, wrestling, and Muay Thai, there are plenty of other martial arts to explore. Judo is a fantastic art and has very effective takedowns, especially against an opponent wearing a jacket or shirt that can be grabbed, which is often the case. Once on the ground, judo has many similarities with Brazilian jiu-jitsu and many of the same techniques are taught. In areas where there might not be any Brazilian jiu-jitsu schools, judo is the next best replacement. The Russian art of SAMBO is also an extremely effective grappling art with an emphasis on leg locks.

There are other martial arts that can be good to look into such as Krav Maga and Systema, both of which focus on self-defense as its primary mission. Martial arts like Escrima and Kali from the Philippines, also known as Arnis, which focus on fighting with sticks and knives. Also, the Dog Brothers have pushed the limit in full-contact weapons sparring—and in that effort have garnered real-world knowledge beyond what was previously available.

The list could go on and on. There is no reason to ever stop training and learning martial arts. Of course, it is good to be prepared to handle a self defense situation, but the benefits of martial arts training go far beyond self-defense.

Of course, you get physically conditioned. You also get mentally tougher—real martial arts are hard. They are a mental and physical grind. If the martial art you are training in is easy, it isn't likely doing you much good. Martial arts also get you used to being in uncomfortable situations and continuing to fight on. This is important in any endeavor. Martial arts will make you better.

So train. Don't think about it. Don't take time to "get in shape" before you start. Just go start. The rest will come...

WHERE

When picking a good jiu-jitsu academy, first things first: Find some schools that are in your immediate area. Proximity is important. The more convenient it is to get to training, the more often you will be able train. So find some schools that are close to your home or work or some other place where it isn't an out-of-your-way gut check to show up and train.

Once you have identified some academies close by, go and pay a visit. The atmospheres in gyms can vary greatly. Some are very traditional, demand matching uniforms, bowing to instructors and to the mat, and are run in a very rigid manner. Other schools do not operate with that tradition. There is no bowing. A wide variety of uniforms can be seen on the mat. Instructors are called by their first names instead of "Master," or "Sensei," or "Professor." I have trained in both these types of schools, I am fine with both, and both types have produced world champions. You may end up preferring one style or another, but when you

TO TRAIN

show up, don't have any preconceived ideas of
what the school will be like.

Also, don't just show up and watch. Bring your
gear and participate. Evaluate the class. How
was it taught? What was the attitude of the
instructor and the other students? Talk to the
students. What are their goals? Are their goals
similar to yours? Was there much ego on the mat?
Did anyone try to rip your head off?

What about the instructor? Depending on where
you live the instructor may or may not be a black
belt. While a black belt instructor is optimal,
some areas of the world just don't have any.
That's okay. A brown belt or a purple belt can
give great instruction as well. There can be some
concern about the legitimacy of the lineage of
the instructor as well. Luckily, the internet has
solved most of that. A quick internet search can
tell you more about the instructor, where they got
their black belt, what competitions they have

won, and how long they have been training. Do some research and even ask some knowledgeable people in the area or on the web. Once you are confident the instructor is legit, assess their personality. Was he or she personable? Did they teach clearly and methodically? Were they having fun?

Also, with regard to the instructor, remember jiu-jitsu is not a religion and a jiu-jitsu instructor is not a god. So, while they deserve respect, just as any other person does, they should give respect as well—even to brand-new white belt students. Jiu-jitsu should not feel like a cult—at all.

Bottom line, jiu-jitsu should be fun, friendly, and engaging. You should look forward to going to jiu-jitsu because you know you will get pushed mentally and physically. While jiu-jitsu will absolutely be humbling, tiring, and frustrating, if you don't enjoy it, you are either letting your ego get in the way, or you are in the wrong school.

IMMEDIATE ACTION DRILLS:

Obviously, training is the best way to prepare to face threats. But there is a difference between a training scenario at the gym or at the range and a real confrontation on the street.

How can you be ready for that? And how should you react? The first thing to do is train. Train hard. Train for worst-case scenarios. Train for things to go wrong by putting yourself in horrible training situations and finding your way out of them. The next most important concept is avoidance. Yes. Avoid the danger. Stay away from high-threat areas.

But we can't always avoid high-threat areas— and sometimes the high-threat area doesn't avoid us. In the world today, conflict and danger can occur anytime and anywhere. So it is important to maintain situational awareness at all times. Pay attention to your surroundings. Look at suspicious people. Look at unsuspicious people. What are they doing? Where are they going? What are they looking at? Assess.

FACING A THREAT

While you assess, think of contingencies.
Where is your closest escape route? Where is
the closest cover and concealment—"cover"
being a place to shield you from bullets and
"concealment" being a place to hide.

If you are maintaining situational awareness, you
should be very hard to surprise. If you sense
something is going wrong or you sense a threat,
proactively move away from it. Walk to the other
side of the street. Accelerate your car. Walk out
the door. Don't wait for things to get worse.

If you do get surprised and you are caught in a
bad situation: **ACT**.

If you can run away from an assailant, do it. If
you can't run because they have a hold on you,
attack them. Put all your training to use as
quickly and as violently as possible. As soon as
you can break free, do it and run.

If shooting starts, get down. Call the police at the first opportunity. If the shooting is single shots being fired at a slower pace, run immediately and keep running. If the shooting is rapid-fire, find some solid cover to get behind. Wait for a lull. When the lull comes, run—that may be your only chance.

If you are trapped in a room with an active shooter outside, barricade yourself. If there is an ideal hiding place, hide. If not, prepare to attack them as soon as they enter the room. Get anyone in the room with you on board and ready to swarm the attacker.

If you are carrying a firearm, use it to eliminate any immediate threat to your life or the life of someone else.

USE EXTREME CAUTION WHEN USING A FIREARM IN ANY
SITUATION: KNOW YOUR TARGET. KNOW THE BACKDROP.
And, recognize that you might not know who is a
good guy and who is a bad guy. The police might
also see you as the threat. Some police officers
might be in plain clothes. So if you confidently
know your target and have to use your weapon, do
it quickly and efficiently. Then put it away and
do your best to identify yourself as a friendly.

FUEL:
FEEDING
THE MACHINE

BALANCE

Homeostasis is the tendency to move toward a state of balance. For instance, in a house, the thermostat keeps the temperature in balance. In the summer it turns on the air conditioner when it gets too hot, and in the winter it turns on the heat when it gets too cold. Homeostasis is being maintained.

• The body also tries to maintain a state of balance in many ways. Like the house, the body maintains a balanced temperature by shivering to heat or sweating to cool.

• Osmoregulation is the regulation of water content in the body. In order to maintain balance, the body uses thirst to increase water levels and sweat and urine to expel excess water.

• The body also uses systems to maintain the balance of acidity, blood pressure, sodium and potassium concentrations in the blood, and plasma ionized calcium. Failure to

maintain the proper balance in
these systems can cause significant
health problems.

There is another balance our bodies
maintain that we have a huge influence
over. It is our blood glucose level,
what we commonly call our blood sugar
level. We can directly influence our
blood sugar levels by what we eat. When
we eat carbohydrates, our blood sugar
levels go up. When we eat a lot of
carbohydrates, our blood sugar levels go
up a lot. The primary action our bodies
take to regulate high blood sugar levels
is to release the hormone insulin into our
blood from the pancreas. Once released,
insulin pushes the sugar in the blood into
fat cells and also slows down the process
of fat in the fat cells being pulled out
and used for energy. Obviously, when your
body is putting fat into fat cells and not
using your fat for energy, you get fatter.

In order to use the fat in your body for energy, the body must have gone through its most readily available source of energy: glucose or sugar in the blood. Once that is depleted, the body begins to utilize fat for energy. You can deplete that sugar in the blood by exercising until it is gone, fasting until it is gone, or adjusting your carbohydrate intake.

There are other extremely negative effects of continued elevated insulin levels in the blood beyond gaining or maintaining body fat. Consistent spiking of insulin in the blood can lead to insulin resistance, which can eventually lead to type 2 diabetes. Other long-term impacts that prolonged elevated insulin levels can cause are heart disease, diabetic retinopathy (blindness), strokes, and kidney failure. Not good.

So, the solution seems obvious:
Stop eating carbohydrates—
or at least minimize
carbohydrate intake.

Why is that so hard? The answer is
simple: Carbohydrates are addictive.
Yes, sugar is like a drug in your brain
and causes neurochemical responses
similar to drugs like heroin.

ADDICTED

Sugar truly is addictive. It stimulates the same
parts of the brain as heroin and cocaine.
When you have it you want more of it.

And you know this to be true.

That's why you can't stop eating it.
And when you do stop eating it, you will feel
withdrawal.
Headache.
Irritation.
Anxiety.
Lies.

TO SUGAR

The lies will come, and they will come from **you**.
The lies you will tell yourself are:
    It's no big deal.
        You can just have a little.
            It isn't worth it to feel *this* bad.
          The body *needs* carbs.
You will rationalize and start to listen to the lies.

DON'T.

Stay strong.
    Get off the sugar train.
      Get off the addiction.

           Stop eating sugar.

FUEL

The modern diet has been around for about 10,000 years.
That is when man figured out how to plant some foods, grow them, harvest them, make them easier to digest, and store them.
These foods were grains: Wheat, rice, corn.
Our bodies have not adapted to eating grains yet.
When we eat grains, they are turned to sugar in our stomachs.
The insulin level spikes and punishes our bodies internally.
So, it is better to eat what we have evolved to eat—that is the diet of Paleolithic man or caveman.
Here is what that diet consists of:

Eat these:
- Beef (preferably grass-fed)
- Poultry (preferably free-range)
- Fish
- Eggs
- Nuts

- Vegetables
- Fungi
- Roots
- Some dairy (full-fat butter, cream, yogurt, cheese)
- Limited fruit

Do not eat these:
- Grains
- Potatoes
- Refined salt
- Refined sugar
- Processed oils (margarine)
- Legumes

Eating a paleo or caveman diet flips the Standard American Diet on its head from a macronutrient perspective. Instead of eating mostly carbohydrates with minimum fat, this diet consists of mostly fat, then protein, and finally minimal carbohydrates.

Some people use the 80/20 rule, meaning they stick with "clean" paleo eating 80% of the time and then the other 20% of the time they eat whatever they want. The problem is that the 80/20 becomes 60/40, then 40/60, then 20/80 and then all bets are off.

Don't follow the 80/20 rule. Follow the 100% rule—that might turn into the 99% rule and that is okay. But the 80/20 rule isn't a rule. It's a step down the slippery slope.

We know sugar is addictive. You are an addict. There is no such thing as an addict who is allowed to use their drug of choice 20% of the time, whether it is alcohol or cocaine or heroin.

You are in the same boat. Going cold turkey and **HOLDING THE LINE** is the best way to stay on track.

Once you have spent enough time staying 100% clean and you are adapted to that method of eating both mentally and physically, you can make some excursions to the dark side. I have an occasional mint chocolate chip milkshake or some other delicious but not nutritious treat.

And I make sure I earn it beforehand with some serious, extreme physical activity.

Over time, you will realize that you have lost your sweet tooth. You will also realize that the aftereffects, the sugar rush, the sugar crash, and the lack of energy the next day, make the excursions to the dark side highly undesirable and will encourage you to **STAY CLEAN.**

I have some treats that make it easier to stay clean. I eat a couple squares of 80%+ dark chocolate dipped in coconut oil. I have a small glass of full cream with a little MCT oil and a dash of chocolate milk powder. Sometimes I'll have whipped cream with nuts on it. If you are on a strict diet, each one of those treats will taste like the richest most satisfying dessert you have ever had.

Now, there are times during travel and work and life when the right foods simply are not available. In an airport or an office party or a restaurant where you are having a business meeting. My solution to that is very simple: Don't eat. It's called a fast, and it is actually very good for you.

FASTING

Newsflash: **YOU DON'T HAVE TO EAT.**

Fasting is a gift. All those times you are at a party or the airport or on a train and they don't have any good, healthy food for you to eat, the answer is simple:

DON'T EAT.

Often, not eating—fasting—is beneficial for you. Here are some of the physiological benefits that fasting appears to bring:
- Improves function of cells, genes, and hormones
- Induces loss of body fat
- Reduces risk of insulin resistance and type 2 diabetes
- Reduces oxidative stress and inflammation
- Induces cell repair processes
- Increases brain-derived neurotrophic factors
- Increases levels of endorphins
- Induces detoxification process

There are also some psychological benefits that
I find very real. First of all, fasting demands
that you exercise your will.
It is not easy.
In this modern age, we are surrounded by food all
day every day.
Your caveman survival instinct, which is afraid
of starving, screams at you:

"Eat that food! Eat as much as you can!
This might be your last chance!"

DON'T FALL FOR THAT.

This isn't the last food you will ever see.
In fact: You will see more food in about
ten minutes.
You don't need it.
You won't die without it.
In fact: Just the opposite is true.
In this age, much of the food around is actually
trying to kill you.

It is poison.
Donuts? Poison. Soda? Poison.
Potato chips? Poison.

YOU DON'T NEED IT.

Another huge benefit of fasting is that it recalibrates your hunger demand signals. We often think we are starving after a few hours without food.
"I haven't had anything to eat since breakfast," we shout at 1:15 in the afternoon. We literally say: "I'm starving!"

YOU ARE NOT STARVING.

Humans can survive thirty days without food.
You can make it a few extra hours.
You can actually make it a few days without any issue.
I fast twenty-four hours fairly regularly.

Fuel: Feeding the Machine

I do seventy-two-hour fasts approximately every three months.
And you know what, they aren't that big of a deal. When I am fasting, I still do everything I would normally do if I were eating. I work. Work out. Train jiu-jitsu.

I drink water, some tea, maybe eat some sunflower seeds in the shell just to have something to chew on. But fasting isn't that hard and you will feel better at the end of it. Fasting will recalibrate what hunger is to you. You will realize that you aren't actually hungry most of the time. You are just bored. And, at the end of a fast, your food will taste better, too.

REPAIR AND MAINTENANCE:

INJURY PREVENTION AND RECOVERY

STRETCHING

Stretching is an important part of being physically fit. It improves range of motion, helps in recovery, and also prevents injuries. There are a multitude of stretching routines out there from ancient forms of yoga to present-day innovations from people like Pavel Tsatsouline and programs like Kelly Starrett's MobilityWOD. Explore those and find the stretches that work best for you. Some basic stretches that I find most useful are: kneeling hip flexor stretch, swimmer stretch, Cossack stretch, hip external rotation stretch, reverse sleeper stretch, couch stretch, downward dog, and the cow face pose.

You can also stretch during your warm-ups and your workouts by ensuring that you use a full range of motion during the exercises, especially during warm-up sets when doing slow repetitions. For instance, when doing a slow squat during warm-up, make sure it is not only slow but also makes it through the entire range of motion of the squat, perhaps even a little further than you might go when performing the exercise with weight. The same thing goes for exercises like dips, push-ups, and pull-ups: When warming up, go slow and go through the entire range of motion, even pushing a little bit past normal at the top and bottom of the exercise.

Like anything else in health and fitness, stretching requires consistency, so figure out what movements are most beneficial for you. Don't pick too many—stretching can be done in as little as ten to fifteen minutes. But it needs to be done, so make it part of your routine.

Then: Stick to your routine.

DEALING WITH

You are going to get injured.
You are going to get sick.
Regardless of how careful you are in your
training, how clean you eat, and how healthy you
live, you are still human.
Injuries and illness will occur.
My theory for overcoming injuries and
illnesses is simple:

DO WHAT YOU CAN.

If you are sick or injured, don't use that as an
excuse to skip workouts or stay in bed all day.

Do what you can.

Hurt your knee? Work your upper body. Work the
good leg. Hurt your shoulder? Time to work on
one-armed pull-ups and push-ups. Focus on your
core and legs until your shoulder heals up.

Tendinitis from using the grip too much? Sounds
like it is time to focus on sprinting and
jumping plyometrics.

INJURIES AND ILLNESS

Got a little cold? Flu? Same thing: **DO WHAT YOU CAN**. Maybe it is just going for a walk. A couple sets of sit-ups and push-ups. But don't just stay in bed all day.

Now, sometimes, you get plain knocked out by illness or a virus. If it is that bad and your body absolutely needs rest, good, listen to your body and **TAKE THE REST**. Also, don't bring your disease to the gym to spread around. Work out at home.

Same thing with injuries. Some injuries prevent you from doing the physical things you like to do. Good. Do what you can, work on some skills that you can do. Pick up a guitar. Write a book. Draw. Paint. Compose a song. Blog. Create. Learn. Do *something*.

Take advantage of physical injuries and sickness by doing something you don't normally have time for. In other words: GET AFTER IT.

THE WORKOUTS

WARMING

Before you start your workout,
you need to get warm.

I like my warm-up to include exercises or
exercises with light weight slowly and
through the entire range of motion. Here is a
nice little warm-up:

Hang on the pull-up bar for 10–15 seconds. Get
in the push-up position and hold it for 10–15
seconds. Drop your hips to the ground and stretch
your abs. Lift your hips to the sky and stretch
your hamstrings and your back. Stand up. Do
a slow squat and sit at the bottom for 10–15
seconds. Do a burpee. Do a few jumping jacks.

Now go back to the bar and do one pull-up.
Drop down and do a push-up, then do a slow dive-
bomber push-up. Stand up and do a slow, full-
range-of-motion squat. Follow that up with a
burpee, then five jumping jacks.

Now repeat the cycle again, doing two repetitions
of each exercise and ten jumping jacks. Then do

UP

the cycle with 3 repetitions of each exercise and
15 jumping jacks. Continue increasing repetitions
until you get to 5 of each exercise and 25
jumping jacks.

That is a solid warm-up; the blood is *flowing*.

If your workout for the day is focused on a
specific movement, do that movement with some
light weights. For instance, if you are doing
deadlifts, do some deadlifts with light weight.
If you are doing clean and jerks, do some clean
and jerks with a PVC pipe or just the bar. If you
are doing squats, do some slow, deep, controlled
squats with a very light weight, perfect form,
and through the complete range of motion. These
will not only get your body warm, but will also
strengthen your muscle memory of the movements.
Once you are warm, loose, and focused, you can
start the workout.

WARNING: DON'T LIFT WEIGHTS THAT ARE TOO HEAVY
FOR YOU OR DO MOVEMENTS WITHOUT PROPER TECHNIQUE
OR YOU WILL GET INJURED.

BEGINNER

PULL

Primary Work: 8 sets of max pull-ups
Gut: 2 minutes of sit-ups
MetCon: Run 400 meters 2 times

Directions: Do as many pull-ups as you can in 8 sets. Allow yourself 2-3 minutes rest between each set.

If you can do dead-hang pull-ups, do as many as you can each set, and then add 3-5 kipping pull-ups to the end of each set without dropping off the bar. If you do drop off the bar at the end of your dead-hang pull-ups, jump back up onto the bar immediately for 3-5 kipping pull-ups and then commence the 2-3 minute rest.

If you can't do any pull-ups at all, then use the ground or a stable box on the ground to jump up and get your chin over the bar. Once your chin is over the bar, hold yourself there as long as you can. This is called a "negative repetition."

PUSH

Primary Work: 8 sets of max push-ups
Gut: 2 minutes of leg-raises, 10-45 degrees
MetCon: Max burpees in 2 minutes

Directions: Do as many push-ups as you can in 8 sets. Allow yourself 2-3 minutes rest between each set.

Vary the width of your hands, anywhere from 6 inches closer than shoulder-width to 6 inches farther apart than shoulder-width.

If you can't do any push-ups at all, try doing them from your knees instead of toes. If even that is difficult, try leaning into a wall and see what you can do there.

SERIES ONE

LIFT
Primary Work: 8 handstand holds
Gut: 2 minutes of V-ups
MetCon: Run 400 meters 2 times, max effort

Directions: Hold the handstand position 8 times. Do not go all the way to muscle failure, but to muscle fatigue. Count how many seconds you hold the position. Allow yourself 2-3 minutes rest between each set.

Use a wall to balance yourself during the handstands. Try not to rely upon it too much.

If you cannot do a handstand at all, get in the push-up position with your feet touching a wall. Walk your feet up the wall and walk your hands closer to the wall. See how close you can get to vertical. Walk your feet and hands back down. Repeat that 8 times.

SQUAT
Primary Work: 50 forward lunges
Gut: 1 minute of crunches, 1 minute of reverse crunches
MetCon: Max burpees in 2 minutes

Directions: Perform 50 forward lunges for each leg, alternating legs with each repetition. Do the lunges in a steady controlled manner. Your knee should brush the ground on each repetition. Time yourself for your records, but the goal is not speed—the goal is controlled lunges at a steady pace. If you reach muscle fatigue, take a 2-3 minute break and then continue. Repeat until you have done the 50 lunges.

BEGINNER

PULL

Primary Work: 5 sets of pull-ups,
maintaining reps
Gut: 2 minutes of sit-ups
MetCon: Run 400 meters 2 times

Directions: For the first-set workout, do your maximum set of pull-ups. If you can do dead-hang pull-ups, do them. If not, do kipping pull-ups. If you can't do kipping pull-ups, do jumping pull-ups or assisted pull-ups. For the remaining 4 sets, do as many pull-ups as you can, and once you drop off the bar, give yourself a 10-15 second rest before jumping up on the bar and doing more pull-ups until you reach the same number of pull-ups that you did in your first max set. This is called a "broken set," meaning you cannot perform the required repetitions, so you take a quick break and then continue. Once you have completed the broken set, take a 2-3 minute rest, then go again until you have completed 5 sets.

PUSH

Primary Work: 5 sets of push-ups, maintaining reps
Gut: 2 minutes of leg-raises, 10-45 degrees
MetCon: 2 minutes of max burpees

Directions: This workout is the same as the Pull workout in this series, but utilizing push-ups instead of pull-ups. For the first-set workout, do your maximum set of push-ups. If you can do full push-ups, do them. If not, do push-ups from your knees. If you can't do push-ups from the knees, do push-ups against the wall. For the remaining 4 sets, do as many push-ups as you can, and

SERIES TWO

once you can't do any more, give yourself a 10-15 second rest and then continue doing more push-ups until you reach the same number of push-ups that you did in your first max set, using the broken set methodology. Once you have completed the broken set, take a 2-3 minute rest, then go again until you have completed 5 sets.

LIFT
Primary Work: 5 handstand negatives
Secondary Work: Arm circles, side, front, overhead
Gut: 2 minutes of V-ups
MetCon: Run 800 meters, once as hard as you can

Directions: Get into the handstand position and lower yourself as slowly as you can. Use a wall to maintain your balance. Once your head reaches the ground, drop your feet to the ground, stand up and rest for 2-3 minutes, then do it again for 5 full repetitions. Once that is complete do 1 minute each of arm circles to the side, to the front, and overhead.

SQUAT
Primary Work: Jump squats, squat thrusts, lunges
Gut: 1 minute of crunches, 1 minute of reverse crunches
MetCon: Run 1 mile

Directions: Set a timer for 3 sets of 20 seconds. Do 20 seconds of jump squats, 20 seconds of squat thrusts, and 20 seconds of lunges. Rest 2 minutes. Repeat this for a total of 3 rounds. Although you are trying to get maximum repetitions, do not sacrifice range of motion or form for increased repetitions.

BEGINNER

PULL

Primary Work: Pull-up pyramid
Gut: 2 minutes of sit-ups
MetCon: 4 x 100-yard shuttle runs

Directions: This workout is recommended when you can do at least 5 pull-ups. Start by doing 1 pull-up. Rest for a bit. Do 2 pull-ups. Rest for a bit. Do 3 pull-ups. Rest for a bit. Continue to increase the number of pull-ups by 1 each set, until you do not beat your previous number. When you miss your previous number, drop off the bar, shake it out quickly, and then get up and complete the set. Now come back down the "pyramid" by decreasing 1 pull-up from the previous set. If you can't do all the pull-ups in a single set to get to the required number, do the required number in a broken set.

If you can do dead-hang pull-ups, do dead-hang; if not and you can do kipping pull-ups, do them. If you cannot do kipping pull-ups, use jumping pull-ups. For this and any pull-up workout, if you can utilize kipping or jumping pull-ups to complete your set without breaking it, do that sometimes. But sometimes drop off the bar, get a quick rest, and then complete the set.

For the shuttle runs, mark a start line and then a line at 5, 10, 15, and 20 yards. Start on the starting line and run to the 5 yard line, touch the line, run back to the start line; repeat this for the 10, 15, and 20 yard lines. Keep your time. Complete 4 sets. Take 2-3 minutes between sets.

PUSH

Primary Work: Push-up pyramid
Gut: 2 minutes of V-ups
MetCon: Run 1 mile, hard

Directions: This workout is recommended when you can do at least 6-10 push-ups. It follows the same pattern as the pull-up pyramid. Start by doing 1 push-up. Rest for a bit. Do 2 push-ups. Rest for a bit. Do 3 push-ups. Rest for a bit. Continue to increase the number of push-ups by 1 each set, until you do not beat your previous number. When you miss your

SERIES THREE

previous number, rest quickly, and then continue with your push-ups until you complete the set. Now come back down the pyramid by one repetition of push-ups per set. If you can't do all the push-ups in a single set to get to the required number, do the required number in a broken set.

If you can't do regular push-ups, do them from the knees. If that is still not achievable, do them on an incline, such as against a wall or with your hands on a table or a bench.

For this and any push-up workout, if you can utilize push-ups from the knees to complete your set without breaking it, do that sometimes. But sometimes take a quick rest, and then complete the set.

LIFT
Primary Work: 4 handstand holds
Secondary Work: Arm haulers
Tertiary Work: Arm circles, side, front, overhead
Gut: Hold a plank for 1 minute
MetCon: 1 squat thrust and 5 jumping jacks repeatedly for 2 minutes for max number of burpees

Directions: Do a handstand hold. Hold until muscle fatigue, not muscle failure. Once complete, do 1 minute of arm haulers, then 1one minute of arm circles for each position: side, front, and overhead. Once complete, rest for about 2-3 minutes and repeat the circuit 3 more times.

SQUAT
Primary Work: 5 sets of 10 squats/5 forward lunges
Gut: 1 minute of crunches, 1 minute of reverse crunches, hold 1-minute plank
MetCon: Run 400 meters 2 times

Directions: Do 10 squats followed by 5 forward lunges for 5 sets. Rest as needed, but try to maintain a steady pace and move through the exercises with minimum rest. Maintaining good form trumps speed. Lunges are performed with 1 repetition for each leg. Run 400 meters, rest 2-3 minutes, then run another 400 meters.

BEGINNER

PULL

Primary Work: 5 sets of pull-up sprints,
1 minute on, 2 minutes rest
Gut: 2 minutes of sit-ups
MetCon: 4 x 100-yard shuttle runs

Directions: This workout is to gain strength and some endurance in your pull-up muscles. Set a timer for 1 minute of work and 2 minutes of rest. During the 1 minute of work, do as many pull-ups as you can. These will likely be broken sets, meaning you will be dropping off the bar to rest even during your work set. Make the rest during the work set as short as possible (5-7 seconds) before jumping back on the bar and continuing to do pull-ups until the minute is complete. Once the minute is over, rest for 2 minutes, then do another minute of pull-ups. Repeat this until you have done 5 sets of pull-ups.

If you can do dead-hang pull-ups, do dead-hang; if not and you can do kipping pull-ups, do them. If you cannot do kipping pull-ups, use jumping pull-ups. You can also utilize all three types of pull-ups to maximize the number of pull-ups you do during the minute of work.

For the shuttle runs, mark a start line and then a line at 5, 10, 15, and 20 yards. Start on the starting line and run to the 5 yard line, touch the line, run back to the start line; repeat this for the 10, 15, and 20 yard lines. Keep your time. Complete 4 sets.

SERIES FOUR

PUSH
Primary Work: 1 minute of push-up sprints and 2 minutes rest for 5 sets
Gut: Hold 1-minute plank
MetCon: 2 minutes of burpees

Directions: Similar to the pull-up sprints, this workout is to gain strength and some endurance in your push-up muscles. Set a timer for 1 minute of work and 2 minutes of rest. During the 1 minute of work, do as many push-ups as you can. These will likely be broken sets, meaning you might have to rest even during your work set. Make the rest during the work set as short as possible (5-7 seconds) before continuing to do push-ups until the minute is complete. Once the minute is over, rest for 2 minutes, then do another minute of push-ups. Repeat this until you have done 5 sets of push-ups.

Once again, for this and any push-up workout, if you have exhausted your push-up muscles, and you can utilize push-ups from the knees to complete your set without breaking it, do that sometimes. But sometimes take a quick rest, and then complete the set utilizing strict push-ups with the feet on the ground.

LIFT

Primary Work: 5 minutes of handstand holds
Secondary Work: Arm haulers
Tertiary Work: Arm circles, side, front, overhead
Gut: 2 minutes of V-ups
MetCon: Run 400 meters 2 times, max effort

Directions: Hold the handstand position for a total of 5 minutes. Do not do this workout if you cannot hold a handstand position for at least 1 minute. If you cannot hold a handstand position for at least 1 minute, go back to the Lift workout in Series 1, 2, or 3.

For this workout go into the handstand position using a wall for balance. Stay there as long as you can without reaching complete muscle failure and falling onto your head. Count the seconds to track how long you stayed up. Repeat sets until you have reached a total amount of 5 minutes in the handstand position.

Once complete, do 1 minute of arm haulers, then 1 minute of arm circles for each position: side, front, and overhead.

SQUAT

Primary Work: 50 forward lunges and 50 squats
Gut: 1 minute of crunches, 1 minute of reverse crunches
MetCon: Max burpees in 2 minutes

Directions: Perform 50 forward lunges for each leg, alternating legs with each repetition. Do the lunges in a steady controlled manner. Your knee should brush the ground on each repetition. Time yourself for your records, but the goal is not speed—the goal is controlled lunges at a steady pace. If you reach muscle fatigue, take a 2-3 minute break and then continue. Repeat until you have done the 50 lunges. Once you have completed 50 lunges, do 50 body-weight squats.

Again, the goal is not speed, but controlled movement with the fullest range of motion you are capable of. If you need to stop and rest, that is fine. Rest for a minute or two, then continue.

If you lose your balance at the bottom of the squat, it may help to put a 2-inch block under your heels during the squat. Over time, you can move down to a 1.5-inch block, then a 1-inch block, then .5-inch block and eventually you will have improved your flexibility and mobility to where you no longer need a block.

INTERMEDIATE

PULL

Primary Work: 8 sets of max pull-ups/chin-ups
Secondary Work: Hang cleans
Tertiary work: Straight-bar reverse curls and curls
Gut: 2 minutes of sit-ups, 2 minutes of leg-raises
MetCon: Run 400 meters 3 times

Directions

- Do a set of maximum pull-ups. Once the maximum has been reached, drop off the bar, rest for 15-20 seconds, then get back on the bar with the chin-up grip and do as many chin-ups as you can. Once both rapid-fire sets are complete, rest for 2-3 minutes and then do your next set. Complete a total of 8 sets. Attempt to use dead-hang pull-ups for sets requiring maximum numbers. If you can get a couple more repetitions with kipping, then do so.
- Do 6 sets of hang cleans, with a weight that allows you to do 3-6 repetitions per set while maintaining good form.
- Once complete, do a set of reverse-grip curls to exhaustion (aiming for 6-10 repetitions), then switch to a normal grip and complete another maximum set. Rest approximately 1 minute, then repeat for a total of 6 sets.
- Gut: Complete 2 minutes of sit-ups and 2 minutes of leg raises.
- MetCon: Complete a 400-meter sprint 3 times.

PUSH

Primary Work: 8 sets of max dips/push-ups
Secondary Work: Hang snatch movement
Gut: 100 V-ups   MetCon: Max burpees in 3 minutes

Directions

- Do a maximum set of dips. Once the maximum has been reached, drop off the dip bars and do a set of maximum push-ups. Rest for 2-3 minutes and then complete the next set. Perform a total of 8 sets.
- Use a PVC pipe to perform the hang snatch. Do 40 repetitions with perfect form.
- Gut: Do 100 V-ups. Break the set if you have to.
- MetCon: Do the burpees. Fast.

SERIES ONE

LIFT
Primary Work: 8 sets of handstand push-ups and deadlifts
Secondary Work: Barbell press
Gut: 4 sets of knees to elbows, max reps
MetCon: 6 x 100-meter shuttle runs

Directions:
• Do 8 sets of maximum handstand push-ups followed by 1 minute of rest followed by deadlift. For the deadlift, utilize a weight you can lift for 6-8 repetitions. You will get fewer repetitions of each exercise the more sets you do. That is okay. Keep form correct to avoid injury, especially with the deadlift.
• Once initial work is done, do some barbell presses with a moderate weight that you can get 4-8 repetitions of. Do 5 sets of presses.
• Gut: For the knees to elbows, hang from a pull-up bar and raise your knees to touch your elbows.
Do the max reps and then rest 2-3 minutes. Perform 4 sets.
• MetCon: Complete 6 sets of 100-meter shuttle runs with 1 minute of rest between work.

SQUAT
Primary Work: Back squats
Secondary Work: Overhead squats
Tertiary Work: Jump squats
Gut: 3-minute plank
MetCon: 2-mile run

Directions:
• Perform 50 back squats with half your body weight. Break up the set as needed to complete the work.
• Perform 50 overhead squats with a PVC pipe.
• Perform 50 jump squats.
• Gut: Hold the plank position for 3 minutes.
• MetCon: Run 2 miles. Run at a good pace to get metabolic conditioning, but also to loosen the legs after the higher-intensity work. Run hard, but not with an all-out effort.

INTERMEDIATE

PULL

Primary Work: 50 dead-hang pull-ups and 100 kipping pull-ups for time
Secondary Work: Cleans
Tertiary Work: Straight-bar reverse curls and curls
Gut: 2 minutes of sit-ups, 2 minutes of leg-raises
MetCon: Max burpee pull-ups in 5 minutes

Directions:
- Complete 50 dead-hang pull-ups followed by 100 kipping pull-ups as quickly as possible. Break up sets as needed to complete.
- Do 6 sets of cleans, with a weight that allows you to do 3–6 repetitions per set while maintaining good form.
- Once complete, do a set of reverse-grip curls to exhaustion (with a weight that allows you to complete 6–10 repetitions), then switch to a normal grip and complete another maximum set. Rest approximately 1 minute, then repeat for a total of 6 sets.
- Gut: Complete 2 minutes of sit-ups and 2 minutes of leg-raises.
- MetCon: Do the maximum number of burpee pull-ups you can in 5 minutes.

PUSH

Primary Work: 50 dips and 100 push-ups for time
Secondary Work: Snatch movement
Gut: 100 V-ups
MetCon: Max burpees in 3 minutes

Directions:
- Do 50 dips followed by 100 strict push-ups in as short a time as possible.
- Use a PVC pipe or an extremely light weight to perform the snatch. Do 40 repetitions with perfect form.
- Gut: Do 100 V-ups. Break the set if you have to.
- MetCon: Do the burpees. Fast.

SERIES TWO

LIFT

Primary Work: 50 handstand push-ups and 50 body-weight deadlifts for time
Secondary Work: Barbell press   **Tertiary Work:** Clean and jerk
Gut: 4 sets of knees to elbows, max reps
MetCon: 6 x 100-meter shuttle runs

Directions:
• Do 50 handstand push-ups followed by 50 deadlifts with your body weight. Keep form correct to avoid injury, especially with the deadlift.
• Once initial work is done, do some barbell presses with a moderate weight that you can get 4–8 repetitions of. Do 5 sets of presses.
• For the clean and jerk, use a PVC pipe or an extremely light weight to practice perfect form for 40 repetitions.
• Gut: For the knees to elbows, hang from a pull-up bar and raise your knees to touch your elbows. Do as many as you can, then rest 2–3 minutes. Perform 4 sets.
• MetCon: Complete 6 sets of 100-meter shuttle runs with 1 minute of rest between work.

SQUAT

Primary Work: 6 max sets of back squats with 100% body weight
Secondary Work: 6 sets of front squats with 50% body weight
Tertiary Work: Overhead squats
Gut: 3-minute plank   **MetCon:** 2-mile run

Directions:
• Complete 6 sets of maximum repetitions of the back squat with your body weight on the bar. Rest 2–3 minutes between each set. Maintain correct form. If form weakens, stop, rest, and move on to the next set.
• Complete 6 sets of maximum repetitions of the front squat with half your body weight on the bar. Again, form is paramount; if your form weakens, your set is complete.
• Perform 50 overhead squats with a PVC pipe or an extremely light weight.
• Gut: Hold the plank position for 3 minutes.
• MetCon: Run 2 miles. Run at a good pace to get metabolic conditioning, but also to loosen the legs after the higher-intensity work. Run hard, but not with an all-out effort.

Discipline Equals Freedom   177

INTERMEDIATE

PULL

Primary Work: 5 sets of L-sit pull-ups, L-tuck pull-ups, dead-hang pull-ups, kipping pull-ups, chin-ups

Secondary Work: Cleans

Tertiary Work: Straight-bar reverse curls and curls

Gut: 2 minutes of sit-ups, 2 minutes of leg-raises

MetCon: 20, 15, 10, 5 of pull-ups/cleans

Directions:

- Do a max set of L-sit pull-ups, rest 15 seconds; do a max set of L-tuck pull-ups, rest 15 seconds; do a max set of dead-hang pull-ups, rest 15 seconds; do a max set of kipping pull-ups, rest 15 seconds; do a max set of chin-ups. Rest 15 seconds and repeat this 5 times.
- Do 4 sets of cleans, with a weight that allows you to do 3-6 repetitions per set while maintaining good form.
- Once complete, do a set of reverse-grip curls to exhaustion (with a weight that allows you to complete 6-10 repetitions), then switch to a normal grip and complete another maximum set. Rest approximately 1 minute, then repeat for a total of 6 sets.
- Gut: Do 2 minutes of sit-ups and 2 minutes of leg-raises
- MetCon: Complete sets of 20, 15, 10, and 5 repetitions alternating between pull-ups and cleans. For the cleans, use the heaviest weight you can without breaking up your sets.

PUSH

Primary Work: 5 sets of dips, clap push-ups, deep push-ups, triceps push-ups

Secondary Work: Snatch movement

Gut: 100 V-ups, 100 Russian twists

MetCon: Max burpees in 3 minutes

Directions:

- Do a maximum set of dips, rest 15 seconds; do a max set of clap push-ups, rest 15 seconds; do a max set of deep push-ups, rest 15 seconds; do a max set of triceps push-ups. Upon completion, rest 2-3 minutes and then repeat this series for 5. For the deep push-ups, simply find a way to elevate your hands off the floor about 6 inches so you can go all the way down in the push-up position to the bottom of the range of motion.
- Use a PVC pipe or an extremely light weight to perform the snatch. Do 40 repetitions with perfect form.
- Gut: Do 100 V-ups followed by 100 Russian twists. Break the sets if you have to.

SERIES THREE

LIFT

Primary Work: 8 max sets of HSPUs (Handstand Push-ups) and 8 sets of body-weight deadlifts
Secondary work: Clean and jerk movement drills
Gut: 4 sets of hanging straight leg-raises, max reps
MetCon: 6 x 100-meter shuttle runs

Directions:
• Do 8 max sets of HSPUs followed by a set of deadlifts with your body weight on the bar. Do not go to complete muscle failure on deadlifts. Instead, go to muscle fatigue and then stop so you can keep form correct to avoid injury.
• For the clean and jerk, use an extremely light weight (approximately 25% of body weight) to practice perfect form for 30 single repetitions.
• Gut: Hang on the pull-up bar and raise your straightened legs as high as you can. Do max reps and then rest 2-3 minutes. Perform 4 sets.
• MetCon: Complete 6 sets of 100-meter shuttle runs with 1 minute of rest between work.

SQUAT

Primary Work: 8 max sets of front squats ~50% body weight
Secondary Work: 3 max sets of back squats ~100% body weight
Tertiary Work: Overhead squat movement
Gut: 3-minute plank   **MetCon:** 2-mile run

Directions:
• Front squat with ~50% body weight for 8 sets. Rest approximately 2 minutes between each set. Do not go to muscle failure, only muscle fatigue. Failure to maintain proper form can result in serious injury.
• Back squat with ~100% body weight for 3 sets. Rest approximately 2 minutes between each set. Maintain proper form and do not go to muscle failure, only muscle fatigue.
• Do 50 overhead squats with a PVC pipe or an extremely light weight.
• MetCon: Run 2 miles at a good pace to get metabolic conditioning, but also to loosen the legs after the higher intensity work. Run hard, but not with an all-out effort.

INTERMEDIATE

PULL

Primary Work: Every Minute On The Minute (EMOTM): pull-up pyramid
Secondary Work: Cleans   Tertiary Work: Straight-bar reverse curls and curls
Gut: 2 minutes of sit-ups, 2 minutes of leg-raises
MetCon: Max burpee pull-ups in 5 minutes

Directions:

• Set a timer for 1 minute. The first minute do 1 pull-up, the second minute do 2 pull-ups, the third minute do 3 pull-ups. Start with dead-hang pull-ups and transition into kipping pull-ups as needed to achieve the required number. Continue to increase the number of pull-ups by 1 each set, until you do not beat your previous number. Complete that number of pull-ups by breaking up the set and finishing. Then come back down the pyramid breaking up sets as needed and resting 1-2 minutes between sets.
• Do 6 sets of cleans, with a weight that allows you to do 3-6 repetitions per set while maintaining good form. Once complete, do a set of reverse-grip curls to exhaustion (with a weight that allows you to complete 6-10 repetitions), then switch to a normal grip and complete another maximum set. Rest approximately 1 minute, then repeat for a total of 6 sets.
• Gut: Complete 2 minutes of sit-ups and 2 minutes of leg-raises.
• MetCon: Do sets of 20, 15, 10, and 5 repetitions alternating between pull-ups and cleans. For the cleans, use the heaviest weight you can without breaking up your sets.

PUSH

Primary Work: On the minute dip pyramid
Secondary Work: On the minute push-up pyramid
Tertiary Work: Snatch movement   Gut: 100 V-ups, 100 Russian twists
MetCon: Max burpees in 3 minutes

Directions:

• Set a timer for 1 minute. The first minute do 1 dip, the second minute do 2 dips, the third minute do 3 dips. Use slow, deep, full-range-of-motion dips. Continue to increase the number of pull-ups by 1 each set, until you do not complete the required number. Complete that number of dips by breaking up the set and finishing. Then come back down the pyramid breaking up sets as needed and resting 1-2 minutes between sets.
• Once dips are completed, do the same thing again, but using strict, full-range-of-motion push-ups.

SERIES FOUR

- Use a PVC pipe or an extremely light weight to perform the snatch. Do 40 repetitions with perfect form.
- Gut: Do 100 V-ups followed by 100 Russian twists. Break the sets if you have to.
- MetCon: Do the burpees. Fast.

LIFT
Primary Work: Tabata body-weight deadlifts followed by Tabata HSPUs
Secondary Work: Clean and jerk movement drills
Gut: 4 max sets of hanging straight leg-raises
MetCon: 6 x 100-meter shuttle runs

Directions:
- For the Tabata protocol, set a timer for 8 sets of 20 seconds of work followed by 10 seconds of rest. Use this protocol to do the max number of deadlift repetitions with body weight on the bar. Strict form is paramount to avoid injury. Once the deadlifts are complete, do the same protocol for HSPUs.
- For the clean and jerks, use an extremely light weight (approximately 25% of body weight) to practice perfect form for 30 single repetitions.
- Gut: Hang on the pull-up bar and raise your straightened legs as high as you can. Do max reps and then rest 2 minutes. Perform 4 sets.
- MetCon: Complete 6 sets of 100-meter shuttle runs with 1 minute of rest between work.

SQUAT
Primary Work: 8 max sets of back squats ~100% body weight
Secondary Work: 3 max sets of front squats ~50% body weight
Gut: 3-minute plank   **MetCon:** 2-mile run

Directions:
- Back squat max reps with ~100% body weight for 8 sets. Rest approximately 2 minutes between each set. Do not go to muscle failure, only muscle fatigue. Keep form right and correct. Failure to maintain proper form can result in serious injury.
- Front squat max reps with ~50% body weight for 3 sets. Rest approximately 2 minutes between each set. Maintain proper form and do not go to muscle failure, only muscle fatigue.
- Gut: Hold the plank position for 3 minutes.
- MetCon: Run 2 miles at a good pace to get metabolic conditioning, but also to loosen the legs after the high-intensity work. Run hard, but not with an all-out effort.

Discipline Equals Freedom   181

ADVANCED

PULL

Primary Work: 5 sets of weighted pull-ups and pull-ups
Secondary Work: Hang cleans   Gut: 100 V-ups, 100 Russian twists
MetCon: 25 pull-ups/run 400 meters x 4

Directions:

• Utilize a weight belt or weight vest of ~20% of your body weight. Complete 5 sets of dead-hang weighted pull-ups, resting 1-2 minutes between each set. Then complete 5 sets of weighted kipping pull-ups, resting 1-2 minutes between each set. Next, remove the weight belt and complete 5 sets of dead-hang pull-ups. Finally do 5 max sets of non-weighted kipping pull-ups.

• Do 6 sets of hang cleans, with a weight that allows you to do 3-6 repetitions per set while maintaining good form.

• Gut: Do 100 V-ups followed by 100 Russian twists.

• MetCon: Do 25 pull-ups, then run 400 meters. Repeat for a total of 4 rounds.

PUSH

Primary Work: Weighted ring-dips, weighted bar-dips
Gut: 5 sets of hanging leg-raises
MetCon: Power snatch/clap push-ups/burpees 20, 15, 10, 5

Directions:

• Utilize a weight belt or weight vest of ~20% of your body weight. Complete 5 sets of weighted ring-dips, resting 1-2 minutes between each set. Then complete 5 sets of weighted bar-dips, resting 1-2 minutes between each set. Next, remove the weight belt and complete 5 sets of ring-dips. Finally, do 5 max sets of unweighted dips.

• Gut: Do 5 sets of hanging leg-raises.

• MetCon: Perform rounds of power snatches, clap push-ups, and burpees with 20, 15, 10, and 5 repetitions as fast as possible. For the power snatches use ~30-40% of your body weight.

LIFT

Primary Work: Snatch, clean and jerk, deadlift
Gut: GHD sit-ups x 100   MetCon: 6 x 100-meter shuttle runs

Directions:

• Form and technique are absolutely critical. Sacrificing proper form will

SERIES ONE

not make you stronger; it will only make you injured. Attending a live,
hands-on coaching program by a professional for these lifts is highly
recommended prior to these workouts. If you cannot perform these lifts
with strict technique and form, DO NOT DO THEM. YOU WILL GET INJURED.

• Begin snatching 3-5 repetitions per weight. Increase weight
toward maximum 5-20 pounds each lift, looking to reach your maximum
in approximately 8 sets. Once you have missed a weight 2 times,
switch to the clean and jerk. Continue to add weight in 5-20 pound
increments until you reach your maximum, which you are trying to do
in approximately 6 sets. Once you have missed 2 clean and jerks,
switch to the deadlift. Continue to add weight in increments of 10-50
pounds until you have reached your maximum. Once you have reached your
maximum, do 2 singles at that weight.

• Gut: Do 100 GHD sit-ups.

• MetCon: 6 x 100-meter shuttle runs

SQUAT

Primary Work: Overhead squat, front squat, back squat
Gut: Hanging leg-raises   MetCon: 2-mile run

Directions:

• Maintain strict form when doing these exercises. Failure to do so
can and will result in serious injury. Do not let your ego dictate the
weight you use.

• Rest approximately 2 minutes between each of these sets. Begin
overhead squats in 3-5 repetitions per weight. Increase weight toward
maximum 5-20 pounds each lift, looking to reach your maximum in
approximately 8 sets. Once you have missed a weight, switch to the front
squat. Continue to add weight in 5-20 pound increments until you reach
your maximum, which you are trying to do in approximately 6 sets. Once
you have missed a front squat, switch to the back squat. Continue to add
weight in increments of 10-20 pounds until you have reached your maximum.
Once you have reached your maximum, do 2 singles at that weight.

• Gut: 5 sets of max hanging leg-raises.

• MetCon: Run 2 miles at a good pace, but not with an all-out effort.
The goal is to loosen the legs after heavy work.

Again: During the lifts, keep form tight and correct.

ADVANCED

PULL

Primary Work: 30 muscle-ups, 100 dead-hang pull-ups, 100 kipping pull-ups for time
Secondary Work: Hang cleans
Tertiary Work: Reverse curls/curls
Gut: 100 V-ups, 100 Russian twists, 100 sit-ups, 100 reverse crunches
MetCon: 20, 15, 10, 5 of pull-ups/cleans

Directions:

• Do 30 muscle-ups, followed by 100 dead-hang pull-ups, followed by 100 kipping pull-ups as fast as possible.
• Do 6 sets of hang cleans, with a weight that allows you to do 3-6 repetitions per set while maintaining good form.
• Complete 5 sets of reverse curls followed by curls, with a weight that allows you to complete 8-12 repetitions.
• Gut: Do 100 V-ups followed by 100 Russian twists.
• MetCon: Perform 4 sets of cleans/pull-ups with these repetitions: 20, 15, 10, 5. Utilize ~60% body weight for the cleans.

PUSH

Primary Work: Ring-dips, dips, ring push-ups, push-ups
Gut: 5 sets of hanging leg-raises
MetCon: 100 burpees for time

Directions:

• Do 100 ring-dips, followed by 100 dips, followed by 100 ring push-ups, followed by 100 regular push-ups as fast as possible.
• Gut: Do 5 max sets of hanging leg-raises.
• MetCon: Complete 100 burpees for time.

SERIES TWO

LIFT

Primary Work: Deadlift   Gut: 100 GHD sit-ups
MetCon: Circuit HSPU, clean and jerk, deadlift

Directions:
• Form and technique are absolutely critical. Sacrificing proper form will
not make you stronger; it will only make you injured. Attending a live,
hands-on coaching program by a professional for these lifts is highly
recommended prior to these workouts. If you cannot perform these deadlifts
with strict technique and form, DO NOT DO THEM. YOU WILL GET INJURED.
• Perform 8-10 sets of deadlift, building up to 4 sets with a
weight that allows you to complete 2-4 repetitions.
• Gut: Do 100 GHD sit-ups.
• MetCon: Set up a bar with ~150% of your body weight, and one bar
with ~60% of your body weight. For time, perform 4 rounds of HSPUs,
clean and jerks with ~60% body weight, and deadlifts with ~150%
body weight with these repetitions: 20, 15, 10, 5.

SQUAT

Primary Work: Back squat
Gut: 100 sit-ups with ~20% body weight on chest
MetCon: Overhead squat/back squat/run

Directions:
• Maintain strict form when doing these exercises. Failure to do so
can and will result in serious injury. Do not let your ego dictate
the weight you use.
• Perform 8-10 sets of back squats, building up to 4 sets with a
weight that allows you to complete 2-4 repetitions.
• Gut: With a plate on your chest of approximately 20% body weight,
perform 100 sit-ups.
• MetCon: For time, perform 4 rounds of overhead squats with ~60%
body weight, followed by back squat with 100% body weight for
repetitions of 20, 15, 10, 5. Run 400 meters between each round.

Again: During the lifts, keep form tight and correct.

ADVANCED

PULL

Primary Work: 3 minutes on 1-minute rest: muscle-ups, L-sit pull-ups, L-tuck pull-ups, dead-hang pull-ups, dead-hang chin-ups, kipping pull-ups

Secondary Work: Hang cleans

Tertiary Work: Reverse curls/curls

Gut: 100 V-ups, 100 Russian twists,

MetCon: 20, 15, 10, 5 of pull-ups/cleans

Directions:

• Set your timer for 3 minutes of work followed by 1 minute of rest. Perform as many muscle-ups as you can in 3 minutes, then rest 1 minute. Repeat the same pattern for L-sit pull-ups, L-tuck pull-ups, dead-hang pull-ups, dead-hang chin-ups, and kipping pull-ups. Once your time is up for kipping pull-ups, continue doing kipping pull-ups until you reach 100.

• Do 6 sets of hang cleans, with a weight that allows you to do 3-6 repetitions per set while maintaining good form.

• Complete 5 sets of reverse curls followed by curls, with a weight that allows you to complete 8-12 repetitions.

• Gut: Do 100 V-ups followed by 100 Russian twists.

• MetCon: Perform 4 sets of cleans/pull-ups with these repetitions: 20, 15, 10, 5.

PUSH

Primary Work: 3 minutes on 1-minute rest: ring-dips, ring push-ups, dips, clap push-ups, deep push-ups, push-ups

Secondary Work: Snatch movement

Gut: 5-minute plank   MetCon: Burpees 3x3

Directions:

• Set your timer for 3 minutes of work followed by 1 minute of rest. Perform as many ring-dips as you can in 3 minutes, then rest 1 minute. Repeat the same pattern for ring push-ups, dips, clap push-ups, deep push-ups, and regular push-ups. Once your time is up for push-ups, continue doing push-ups until you reach 100.

• Do 40 repetitions of the snatch movement with an extremely light weight.

• Gut: Hold the plank position for 5 minutes.

SERIES THREE

- MetCon: Perform 3 rounds of max burpees in 3 minutes with 1 minute of rest between rounds.

LIFT
Primary Work: Clean and jerk   **Gut: 100 GHD sit-ups**
MetCon: Circuit HSPUs, clean and jerks, deadlifts

Directions:
- Form and technique are absolutely critical. Sacrificing proper form will not make you stronger; it will only make you injured. Attending a live, hands-on coaching program by a professional for these lifts is highly recommended prior to these workouts. If you cannot perform these lifts with strict technique and form, DO NOT DO THEM. YOU WILL GET INJURED.
- Perform 8-10 sets of the clean and jerks, building up to 4 sets with a weight that allows you to complete 2-4 repetitions.
- Gut: Do 100 V-ups followed by 100 Russian twists holding 10-25 pounds.
- MetCon: Set up a bar with ~180% of your body weight, and a bar with ~80% of your body weight. For time, perform 10 rounds of HSPUs, clean and jerks with ~80% body weight, and deadlifts with ~180% body weight with these repetitions: 10, 9, 8, 7, 6, 5, 4, 3, 2, 1.

SQUAT
Primary Work: Overhead squat, front squat, back squat
Gut: 100 sit-ups with ~20% body weight on chest   MetCon: Run

Directions:
- Maintain strict form when doing these exercises. Failure to do so can and will result in serious injury. Do not let your ego dictate the weight you use.
- Perform 50 overhead squats with ~60% body weight. Perform 50 front squats with ~80% body weight. Perform 50 back squats with body weight.
- Gut: With a plate on your chest of approximately 20% body weight, perform 100 sit-ups.
- MetCon: Run 2 miles at a decent pace.

Again: During the lifts, keep form tight and correct. Form is paramount. If form starts to slip, go lighter in weight.

ADVANCED

PULL

Primary Work: Muscle-ups, L-sit pull-ups, L-tuck pull-ups, dead-hang pull-ups, kipping pull-ups, dead-hang chin-ups

Secondary Work: Hang cleans

Tertiary Work: Reverse curls/curls

Gut: 100 V-ups, 100 Russian twists, 100 sit-ups, 100 reverse crunches

MetCon: Every Minute On The Minute (EMOTM): burpees/pull-ups

Directions:

• Perform as many muscle-ups as you can in one set. Next do a set of max L-sit pull-ups, then max L-tuck pull-ups, max dead-hang pull-ups, max kipping pull-ups, and finally max chin-ups. Repeat this circuit 5 times, taking minimal rest between sets.

• Do 6 sets of dead-hang chin-ups, with a weight that allows you to do 3-6 repetitions per set while maintaining good form.

• Complete 5 sets of reverse curls followed by curls, with a weight that allows you to complete 8-12 repetitions.

• Gut: Perform 100 each of V-ups, Russian twists, sit-ups, and reverse crunches.

• MetCon: On the minute, perform 5 burpees and then maximum pull-ups for a total of 6 minutes.

PUSH

Primary Work: Ring-dips, ring push-ups, bar-dips, clap push-ups, deep push-ups, push-ups

Secondary Work: Hang snatches

Gut: Ring L-sits

MetCon: On the minute: burpees/ring-dips.

Directions:

• Perform as many ring-dips as you can in one set. Next do a set of max ring push-ups, then max bar-dips, max clap push-ups, max deep push-ups, and finally max regular push-ups. Repeat this circuit 5 times, taking minimal rest between sets.

• Do 6 sets of hang snatches, with a weight that allows you to do 3-6 repetitions per set while maintaining good form.

• Gut: Complete 5 max sets of ring L-sits.

• MetCon: On the minute, perform 5 burpees and then maximum ring-dips for a total of 6 minutes.

SERIES FOUR

LIFT
Primary Work: Clean and jerk
Gut: Complete 5 sets of hanging windshield wipers.
MetCon: Circuit HSPUs, clean and jerks, deadlifts

Directions:
• Form and technique are absolutely critical. Sacrificing proper form will
not make you stronger; it will only make you injured. Attending a live,
hands-on coaching program by a professional for these lifts is highly
recommended prior to these workouts. If you cannot perform these lifts
with strict technique and form, DO NOT DO THEM. YOU WILL GET INJURED.
• Perform 8-10 sets of the clean and jerks, building up to 4 sets with
a weight that allows you to complete 2-4 repetitions.
• Gut: Complete 5 sets of hanging windshield wipers.
• MetCon: Perform 30 repetitions of clean and jerks with ~60% body weight
without putting the bar down, rest 2 minutes; perform 20 repetitions with
the same weight, rest 2 minutes; perform 10 repetitions.

SQUAT
Primary Work: Overhead squat, back squat
Gut: 100 sit-ups with ~20% body weight on chest   MetCon: Run

Directions:
• Maintain strict form when doing these exercises. Failure to do so
can and will result in serious injury. Do not let your ego dictate the
weight you use.
• Perform 8-10 overhead squats, increasing weight each set until you reach
failure. Rest 2-3 minutes between sets. Once failure is reached, drop the
weight back down to the last weight you made and perform 3 more max sets.
• Once overhead squats are complete, add ~20% to that weight. This
weight should be a weight that you can back squat about 10 times. Now
perform 20 back squats without racking the bar. This should be the most
brutal set of squats you have ever done. From repetition 12 on, each
rep should require total focus, concentration, grit, and pure will.
• Gut: With a plate on your chest of approximately 20% body weight,
perform 100 sit-ups.
• MetCon: Run 2 miles at a decent pace.

Again: During the lifts, keep form tight and correct. Form is
paramount. If form starts to slip, go lighter in weight.

Discipline Equals Freedom   189

ROAD WARRIOR

Many jobs require travel. Travel can make working out difficult.

BUT IT DOESN'T MAKE IT IMPOSSIBLE.

There are many ways to get good workouts on the road.

Now. If you are going to a location for an extended period of time, such as a military deployment, it is important to plan ahead to either bring or have access to the right equipment so you can continue working out. In the civilian sector, if you are going to spend an extended amount of time in an area, this might mean joining a local gym.

Whether you bring equipment, utilize someone else's, or join a local gym, it is almost always possible to set up or gain access to some kind of solid workout area and stay on the program.

WORKOUTS

Traveling for shorter time periods, for one to four days at a time, can sometimes cause more disruption than long trips. The difficulty in bringing gear while traveling is one issue because checking bags is a gamble and time consumer in an already compressed schedule.

So. When I travel, I travel light. I carry a chalk bag with chalk, wristbands, a notebook to track my workout, and some one-inch tubular nylon and a hard ball (slightly larger than a lacrosse ball) for doing mobility and maintenance work.

If the hotel has a gym, I get in there and use it. Of course, hotel gyms are usually pretty pathetic. They don't have very heavy weights, they might not have a pull-up bar or a dip bar, and they are generally small. But I get in there and improvise. I will do what I can to reproduce my real workout. Due to a lack of weight, my workout usually consists of lower weights and higher reps. If there is any kind of pull-up bar,

I utilize it. If not, sometimes I will hang a towel over one of the machines in the gym and do pull-ups on that. Many times I have done dips between two treadmills. I will use benches to jump over or on, jump ropes to push the heart rate up, and any other object they have in the gym that I can use to get my blood flowing.

I consider these workouts more of a maintenance routine than a workout that will result in serious progression.

Sometimes, the hotel doesn't have a gym or it is just worthless, or I have a very tight schedule and don't have much time. In those cases, I often just do a hotel room workout on the floor.

The hotel room workouts are rudimentary and, again, are usually not geared toward any great advancement in my physical conditioning. They are more focused on maintaining the discipline of working out early, and getting the benefits that come from working out: blood flow to the brain, releasing endorphins, and overall kick-starting my day. Also, I do try to plan my schedule to do several days' worth of

murderous physical training before I go on the
road so that my body is in need of a rest, and
I can use some simple workouts for recovery.

That being said, I have some quick workouts to
keep me on track when I am on the road.

For a pull workout, I will try to find some kind
of pull-up bar. Usually I can find one in the
hotel parking garage (make sure they are solid!)
or outside on a tree or a piece of scaffolding or
anything that might work. Then I will do 8—10 sets
of pull-ups in a very slow, controlled, dead-hang
manner focusing on the negative—coming down slow.
I might also do various types of pull-ups: chin-
ups, chest-to-bar, typewriter, and countless other
variations. If I need to get the blood flowing, I
will do some burpee pull-ups and some gut.

For a push workout in the hotel room I will
do push-ups—lots of them. Reps of 80, 70, 60,
50, 40, 30, 20, 10. Another variation is reps
of 10, 10, 10, 10, 10, 100, 50, 50, 33, 33,
33, 25, 25, 25, 25, 20, 20, 20, 20, 20, 10,
10, 10, 10, 10. On top of that I will do some
burpees—100 for time. And of course some gut.

For lift day, I will do handstand push-ups, 8–10 max sets, I will mix in some arm haulers, some jumping jacks, arm circles, and of course...burpees.

If I end up in a hotel room for squat day, there are plenty of options. One I like to do is pistols (one-legged squats) and jump squats. I will do 10 pistols each leg, then 20 jump squats; then I do 9 pistols each leg and 18 jump squats; then 8 and 16 right on down to 1 pistol each leg and 2 jump squats. Other possibilities are lunges, split jumps, mountain climbers, squat thrusts, and, yes, burpees.

If I am really sore and need a recovery day, I will do some good stretching, a little gut, some drills from MobilityWOD, with 100 burpees mixed in to get the blood going.

Like I said, most of these routines are more about maintaining fitness on the road for a couple of days, getting the blood flowing to wake up and be alert, and maintaining my discipline.

If I need a real workout, I will simply increase the volume of any of these hotel workouts. Any one of these workouts can become vicious when volume and intensity are turned up. I have destroyed myself many times in hotel rooms all over the world. It just takes some creativity and, of course, **WILL**.

So. When you are on the road. Don't get lazy. Don't get complacent. Don't use the road as an excuse.

Get creative. Get *aggressive*. Get it *done*. When you are on the road,

STAY ON THE PATH.

CONTINUED

There is much more out there than
what I have covered.

Check out kettlebells. They are an outstanding
way to get in shape. Swings, snatches, goblet
squats, high-pulls, lunge-presses, Turkish get-
ups, weighted pull-ups, push-ups with rows—the
list is infinite. Add them to your game to get
it on. Use them to supplement your workouts or do
some all-kettlebell days.

There are also an unbelievable number of
movements that can be taken from gymnastics. The
muscle-up is a staple of my workouts, and it is

IMPROVEMENT AND EXPLORATION

a basic movement in gymnastics. Other moves
like hanging leg-lifts, L-sits, V-ups, front
and back levers, all kinds of multi-plane
pushes and presses. The list goes on and on.
Find a gym or a coach or an online program to
start getting after some of the hardest body-
weight exercises in the world.

And don't stop with kettlebells and gymnastics.
Keep looking. Keep *experimenting*. Keep **exploring**.
Keep getting better.

DO

Appendix: The Workouts

Don't just read this book.
Don't just listen to the podcast.
Don't just watch videos online.

Don't just take notes.
Don't just study them.
Don't just share them with your friends.

Don't just plan.
Don't just mark your calendar.
Don't just "get motivated."

Don't just talk.
Don't just think.
Don't just dream.

No. None of that matters.

The only thing that matters is that you actually do.

SO:

DO.